E UI

Traces of Light

Traces of Light

Sermons and Bible Studies

Gerd Theissen

SCM PRESS LTD

0 334 02629 6

First British edition published 1996 by
SCM Press Ltd, 9–17 St Albans Place,
London N1 0NX

Typeset by The Harrington Consultancy Ltd
and printed in Great Britain by Biddles Ltd, Guildford
and King's Lynn

To the Parish of Sexau,

in gratitude for the award of its Theology Prize, 1993

Contents

Preface   1

'You Shall Not Commit Adultery!'   3
A moral sermon against moralism
  (Exodus 20.14)

Protecting the Stranger and Xenophobia   12
An ugly contradiction in the Bible and in life
  (Exodus 23.1–13)

The Working of the Holy Spirit in Judaism   30
The Old Testament Pentecost story
  (Numbers 11.1–35)

Seduction to Life   47
A woman's story from a male perspective
  (The Book of Ruth)

The Transformation of Complaints and
  Laments into a Confession of Guilt   63
  (Psalm 51.1–15)

Life – A Hymn to God in the Face of Death   69
  (Psalm 118.17–19)

Dreams, Stars and the Distinction between False and
  True Prophecy   73
  (Jeremiah 23.16–29)

'Blessed are the Poor in Spirit'   83
The First Beatitude between the left and right wings of
  Protestantism
  (Matthew 5.3)

Traces of Light   92
Being the light of the world is uncomfortable
   (Matthew 5.3)

Carefree Birds and Lilies and
   Our Anxieties About Them   100
   (Matthew 6.25–34)

The Power of Consensus   105
   or, Can Church Discipline be Humane?
   (Matthew 18.15–20)

'What you have done for the least of my brothers...'   110
Justice in an unjust world
   (Matthew 25.31–46)

Jesus and Hippocrates   127
The end of anxiety about demons
   (Mark 9.14–29)

'You aren't rubbish, you're seeds!'   144
My grandmother's wisdom
   (Luke 8.4.8)

Worshipping God in Spirit and in Truth   154
The mysticism of the Gospel of John and
   the dialogue of the religions
   (John 4.1–41)

The Dream of a Life that does not Live at   173
   the Cost of Other Life
   (Romans 5.8)

Is Paul's Criticism of the Law Anti-Jewish?   177
   (Romans 9.1–5; 9.30–10.4)

Marriage between Cornflakes and God   186
A marriage sermon
   (Romans 5.8)

Contents

The Sympathetic Sides of the Catholic Understanding of
  Marriage   192
A sermon at an ecumenical wedding
  (Romans 15.7)

Everyday Conflicts and God's Longing for the Human
  Being   198
  (James 4.1–10)

Music – A Parable of God   207
A sermon at a music service
  (I Corinthians 4.1–5)

Art as Sign Language of Faith   215
Theological meditations on the Heidelberg window designs of
  Johannes Schreiter

Preface

Why 'Traces of Light'? In the biblical tradition the metaphor of light has a clear significance. God is light. In God's light we see light. These sermons and Bible studies seek to illuminate life, society and the world with God's light. They will have achieved their aim if a trace of this light shines out in hearers and readers.

In calling these texts 'Traces of Light' I am associating this basic significance of the metaphor even more directly with them, first of all as a wish that guided me while I was working on them. I often wanted my sermons to bring light, or at least a tiny trace of light, into darkened lives. I often had specific people and problems in view. I was happy when I suspected that a spark had leapt across – even if this was only a small, glimmering spark.

Furthermore, for me 'light' is an image of enlightenment. There is 'light' in any constructive thinking on basic questions of life. Emotional impulses pass, thoughts remain. Thoughts enter into our inner human dialogue. They have an effect. Constructive thoughts are the presupposition for positive feelings and moods. Therefore I have spent a long time in thought while preparing some of these themes, even if only a small selection of this thought has gone into the sermons: just what was important for dealing constructively with the problems addressed.

'Traces of light' also suggests 'traces'. Here I am thinking of following traces, tracks leading somewhere. Where traces of light are discovered in life, life is given orientation. Possible goals for action become visible. I have always avoided direct appeals. They patronize hearers. They anger the best of them, who are thinking along the same lines. But sermons may and should communicate basic guidelines, and they should do so clearly.

Traces of Light

The phrase 'traces of light' is a metaphor which I have developed in this preface to give a short description of how these sermons and Bible studies came into existence. I have adopted a similar procedure in many texts. Metaphors and images are open, ambiguous, flexible. Therefore they usefully serve in texts as leitmotifs, to break them up or to make points.

This collection contains three closely related genres. The shorter sermons, which one might call 'devotions', were usually given at Wednesday morning worship in St Peter's Church, Heidelberg. This took place at 7 a.m. and was continued with a communal breakfast. The longer sermons were given – often in an abbreviated form – in the same church at Sunday worship. The Bible studies were written for Kirchentags in the Ruhr in 1991 and in Munich in 1993. These more extended texts make it possible to reflect thoughtfully and play with form and imagination to a greater degree than is possible in the shorter texts. However, in my view, they are not greatly different from sermons.

I am grateful to all those who helped in the preparations for this book. Erhard J. Wiedenmann read the proofs and researched the details given in the notes. Wega Schmidt-Thomée and Helga Wolf produced clean versions of the various drafts of the manuscript. Above all I am grateful to those who listened to the sermons and Bible studies – both for their positive response and for their criticism.

The book is dedicated to the parish of Sexau in gratitude for the theology prize which they awarded me.

Heidelberg, September 1993   Gerd Theissen

You Shall Not Commit Adultery!

A moral sermon against moralism

(Exodus 20.14)

Among the Ten Commandments, the prohibition against adultery occupies a special place. This is clear from the following story:

'Mr Meyer goes to the rabbi. "Rabbi," he complains, "someone has stolen my umbrella, my new umbrella. It must be someone in my family: my brother-in-law, my mother-in-law, the *au pair*, perhaps even my father or my own brother. It's intolerable! A thief in one's own family!"

The rabbi reflects. Then he says, "Listen carefully, Meyer. Invite all the family to coffee and biscuits. And when they have drunk your coffee and eaten your biscuits, get out the 'good book' and light the candles. Read the Ten Commandments slowly. And when you get to the Eighth Commandment, 'You shall not steal', then look round at everyone out of the corner of your eye: your brother-in-law, your mother-in-law, the *au pair*, your father, your mother, and you will see – the thief will give himself away."

Two days later Meyer returns with shining eyes and reports: "It was splendid, rabbi, just as you predicted. After the coffee and biscuits, I lit the candles and read the Ten Commandments from the Good Book: to my brother-in-law, my mother-in-law, the *au pair*, my father and my brother. And when I got to the Seventh Commandment, 'You shall not commit adultery', it occurred to me where I left my umbrella.'

We're all like Meyer. We like to use the Ten Commandments for making moral reflections on other people. But the Seventh (or in other ways of counting, the Sixth) Commandment directs us to ourselves. It is a signpost with four arms, and on each of them we read 'Yourself'.

The first arm points to the insight 'No one is perfect, including you'. Not even theologians. Not even the two greatest systematic theologians of this century, Karl Barth and Paul Tillich. They were anything but model husbands. The former lived in a permanent threesome; and in this respect, too, the latter lived on the limit, between marriage and promiscuity. We can see personal tragedy in both cases. They gave an authentic exegesis of the Seventh Commandment in their lives. And their exegesis is simply, 'We are always sinners'.

That is also confirmed by empirical research into behaviour. We read the Kinsey Report from the 1940s almost with nostalgia. At that time twenty per cent of married women aged thirty-five indicated that they had already been unfaithful once. In the 1980s, the number was already fifty per cent. With men the figures are far, far higher.

No wonder, say the sociobiologists: in evolutionary terms marriage is a successful strategy for spreading one's own genes – more rewarding for men than for women, who can already aim at maximal success in propagation with a single partner.

No wonder, say the ethnologists: of the roughly 850 known human societies, only sixteen per cent recognize monogamy as a norm. Lifelong fidelity to one partner is of itself a rather improbable commandment. Putting it into practice is even more improbable.

No wonder, say we theologians. Human beings are carved from crooked wood. Let the one without sin cast the first stone! The one who provocatively suggested that was one hundred per cent certain even without empirical research that no one has the right to cast a stone – no one! Even only a ninety-nine per cent certainty would have been a fatal risk!

No wonder, when we read how this commandment is made even more radical in the Sermon on the Mount: 'Whoever looks on a woman to desire her has already committed adultery in his heart!' Even the most faithful marriage partners often dwell on others in their sexual fantasies, by day or by night. That shouldn't shock or disturb anyone. It's normal.

Doubtless there are many incontrovertible and wise arguments that say that human beings are not born to be faithful in marriage. That makes all the greater the riddle why the obligation to fidelity nevertheless speaks to us so strongly. Why do we hear the imperative 'You must be faithful', contrary to the tendencies of our behaviour? Or am I the only one to experience it like this – conditioned by my old-fashioned feelings and thought-world?

That brings me to the second arm on the signpost. That too points to us. It points the way to the insight that in the Seventh Commandment we always begin with ourselves, with our own quite personal experiences, with our feelings, desires and transgressions. We occupy them as we do our own skin. People who shape their marriage by the slogan 'Join battle!' find it difficult to imagine what a peaceful partnership can be like. With all the weight of their experience they craftily ask the others, 'Well, what problems have you swept under the carpet?' Because we are all imprisoned in our personal experiences, we can quickly hurt others if we talk of marriage and partnership. That makes me hesitate over every word today!

Perhaps I have already hurt someone by emphasizing the normality of adultery. Doesn't this trivialize a great human tragedy?

I'm thinking of those among us who once suffered by seeing a partner turning to someone else. That left deep wounds. There were the tormenting questions: Am I worthless? Aren't I attractive enough?

I'm thinking of those among us who are caught in the middle between two much-loved friends. Those who have to endure this conflict are often very sympathetic people.

But I'm also thinking of those for whom life with their partner is a torment. There are marriages (and also many free partnerships), for which the Seventh Commandment ought to have run, 'You shall not enter into any marriage or partnership which has to be broken.'

To all such people I would like to say something helpful – and also to those who have no partner or have a failed relationship behind them. I am aware that if all the people gathered in this church were to bring their experiences together, there would be a great flood of suffering. Our rafts of relationships float on this flood, are swept to the bank of life and become the flotsam of unhappiness. But precisely when I am drowning in this stream, it becomes all the more marvellous that in it there are also successful relationships. Why do they radiate so much warmth and light? Why are we glad when we feel that two people are happy together? Why are we fascinated when fidelity is lived out, when it becomes an indicative which is taken for granted? Why are we disturbed that it is required as an imperative? Sometimes I ask myself whether anything at all helpful can be said on this topic by expounding a commandment from ancient times. Wouldn't it be more important to understand, to sympathize, to share in the suffering – and also to share in the rejoicing? Are imperatives in place at all here? Doesn't confrontation with an alien 'You shall!' prematurely destroy the conversation?

That brings us to the third arm of the signpost pointing to ourselves. In a world in which everything is already governed by norms and regulations, we long for a sphere that we ourselves determine, in which no public, no state, no church, no neighbours have a say. In marriage and partnership we want to give ourselves norms and obligations. We want to determine the forms of our relationships ourselves – as marriage or as partnership, temporary or long-term, homosexual or heterosexual. The variety of forms of life compels us to make a choice. We are forced to choose.

A glance at history shows us that there are no necessary

forms of life. What is immoral today was moral yesterday. Had Karl Barth been an Old Testament patriarch, his relationship in a threesome would have been regarded as legitimate. Polygamy was allowed at that time. The Seventh Commandment originally did not exclude a relationship with two wives.

Paul Tillich, too, would have been in a better position, to the degree that he had relationships with unmarried women. In the Old Testament that was not regarded as adultery. Adultery was only an invasion of someone else's marriage.

It was only a later development in Judaism, which came to a climax and was recorded in the New Testament, that led to an understanding of the Seventh Commandment as an obligation to life-long mutual fidelity between two partners in a marriage – excluding all other sexual relationships. From a historical perspective that is both improbable and risky. Some people think that this experiment in exclusive, mutual fidelity has already failed.

I'm sceptical about that. But there is no disputing the fact that today various forms of life exist side by side. And many people doubt whether binding norms for all forms of life can be formulated at all. The Seventh Commandment must be re-formulated along the line taken by the feminist theologian Elga Sorge, who turns this commandment into two opposite permissions:

'You may commit adultery. You cannot do otherwise, since any woman who looks on another man to desire him has already committed adultery in her heart. But of course you may also be faithful!'

What are we to say to that? May one be faithful? Or should one be faithful? I am disturbed that both statements have been formulated independently of the consent of the partner in question. For no matter in what forms of life we live, there is one command for all of us, which runs: 'Be faithful to what you have mutually entered into.'

There are couples who have agreed to remain faithful socially, but to allow each other sexual freedom. That, too, is a commitment to fidelity. I don't want to encourage anyone to try anything like that. It's too risky. And often partners have taken on too much in making such agreements.

There are other couples who have parted company, but whose fidelity consists in not spoiling the memories of the others, not giving up knowledge entrusted to them, caring for the children they share.

And finally there are people who have agreed to remain faithful to each other until death divides them. It's a good thing that many of us belong to their number.

The decisive thing is not the abstract formulation which is framed as a norm or permission, as an absolute 'You shall' or 'You may'. The decisive thing is what we have agreed with our particular partner. Thus traditional marriage can also become a mutually free obligation. That is why twenty-two years ago my wife and I chose for our marriage the saying 'All is yours, but you are Christ's'. By 'All is yours', we wanted to say: our marriage is an expression of our decision. We have chosen this form of life, knowing that there are other forms of living together.

But of course we also wanted to say more. A church marriage is more than a public announcement of a commitment. But what is this more? What points beyond our decision? The fourth arm on the signpost points to that.

The Seventh Commandment wants us to remain true to ourselves and constantly to renew the covenant with life.

I know that I am interfering indiscreetly in an inner dialogue which we all carry on secretly with ourselves. I can only speak for myself, from my life and my experiences. And here I often say to myself:

We did not seek out this life. We were born without our agreement. Without our agreement we received these parents and no others, this body and no others. After that we have to say yes to ourselves – somewhere, and time and again, between cradle and grave, between our cry at our birth and the silence of death. This Yes is a response to the will of the Creator. Nowhere do I experience the Creator's will so directly as in this Yes to life. I feel it struggling with other forces, with the forces of death and despair.

That is why this Yes is often only a stubborn, laboured, unreconciled Yes. But there is an experience in which it turns into a reconciled Yes: the experience of love. Such love has many forms. Sexuality and marriage are only a particularly intense form – one of many opportunities of turning a defiant Yes into a reconciled Yes.

Once again: we could not choose ourselves. But we have chosen our partners. We had to accept our bodies and we remain bound to them all our lives. We can accept our partner time and again, body and soul. And we can make all the tendernesses of the body convey a message which keeps saying only one thing, 'Yes.' Yes to a life which is freely bound up with ours – and which belongs to us as indissolubly as our own body.

Once again: we have not chosen ourselves. But we have chosen our partner and were chosen by our partner. Someone gives us to understand, 'I say Yes to the whole of you as you have now become, so contrary and so remarkable.' That is an opportunity for us to turn the defiant Yes to life, which is a Yes to many blind necessities, into a reconciled Yes – a Yes in freedom through love.

Such a Yes can bind us before God until death separates us. You only have to ask yourself, 'Can you affirm the other as intensely as you affirm yourself? Do you feel the power to endure the unavoidable crises in life in relationship to this other and to cope with them as crises in relation to yourself? Do you have the will to affirm the other voluntarily, as you keep having to affirm yourself, all your life? Are you as tolerant of the other as you have to be of yourself if you want to put up with yourself? Are you ready to work as steadily on your relationship to the other as you work on yourself – all your life?

If you have said this Yes and keep saying it every day, then it is an echo of the great Yes which God has inscribed on our existence and which we never completely decipher in our lifetime. Certainly it is an incomplete Yes, but it is an echo of the divine Yes. Certainly it is not an unconditional Yes, but it is a reflection of an unconditional Yes.

We must all accept that relationships can fail. That shouldn't be suppressed. But you should know that something of yourself fails with them. Once you become aware of that, you will not break off a marriage lightly, or enter into a relationship or break one off. You will have to go through a deep crisis if that relationship nevertheless fails. It is like death. But your Yes to yourself will be renewed. For it is not just grounded in you and in the other. It is the echo of a greater Yes which you heard before you could answer. You have been allowed to pass it on incomplete to someone else, and receive it from that other person. But it applies to you for ever, quite independently of this. For before you allied yourselves with another person, God made a covenant with you – an irrevocable covenant for life.

However, when it comes to this covenant we are often just like Meyer. We come to God and complain – not that we have lost an umbrella, but worse, that we have lost ourselves. That we are remote from ourselves. We accuse circumstances. We accuse our bodies, our parents, teachers, fellow human beings. Perhaps we should do as Meyer did and bring out the 'Good Book'. In it you can read of the dialogue between God and human beings, of how God constantly woos them, of God and an adulterous and stubborn generation:

You can read of people who often humiliate and hurt themselves in their relationships.

Of people who are unfaithful and who fail in their relationships.

With such people God makes a covenant for life, with people like Paul Tillich and Karl Barth, with people like you and me.

With people who according to scientific insights are born to unfaithfulness.

With people who nevertheless through love and faithfulness escape and get away from the calculations of sociobiologists and ethnologists.

Every year that you remain faithful you have taken a tiny step from the realm of necessity into a realm of freedom. In so doing you are following the call of God, who wants to free you from any house of slavery, and also from your own unfaithful-

10

ness and unreliability. You will often limp and lag on this way. You will mutter and fail. But don't despair! For God has made a covenant of life with you which will not be revoked. God is speaking to you in his 'good book'. And he is not speaking to imaginary people, but is speaking to people who really exist, when he tells us all:

'Mountains shall move and hills shall fall, but my grace shall not depart from you and the covenant of my peace shall not fail.'

May this peace of God which surpasses all our understanding keep your hearts and minds in Christ Jesus, Amen.

This sermon was given in St Peter's Church, Heidelberg, on 24 June 1990, in a series on the Ten Commandments. The official Barth literature tends to keep quiet about Karl Barth's triangular relationship, whereas Paul Tillich's life is much more openly discussed.

Protecting the Stranger and Xenophobia

An ugly contradiction in the Bible and in life

(Exodus 23.1-13)

You shall not spread a false report. You shall not join hands with the wicked to act as a malicious witness. You shall not follow a majority in wrongdoing; when you bear witness in a lawsuit you shall not side with the majority so as to pervert justice; nor shall you be partial to the poor in a lawsuit. When you come upon your enemy's ox or donkey going astray, you shall bring it back. When you see the donkey of one who hates you lying under its burden and you would hold back from setting it free, you must help to set it free. You shall not pervert the justice due to your poor in their lawsuits. Keep far from a false charge, and do not kill the innocent and those in the right, for I will not acquit the guilty. You shall not oppress a resident alien; you know the heart of an alien, for you were aliens in the land of Egypt.

For six years you shall sow your land and gather in its yield; but the seventh year you shall let it rest and lie fallow, so that the poor of your people may eat; and what they leave the wild animals may eat. You shall do the same with your vineyard, and with your olive orchard. Six days you shall do your work, but on the seventh day you shall rest, so that your ox and your donkey may have relief, and your homeborn slave and the resident alien may be refreshed. Be attentive to all that I have said to you. Do not invoke the names of other gods; do not let them be heard on your lips.

The Sinai narrative is the story of the making of a covenant. God makes men and women his covenant partners, to put his righteousness into practice. Moreover he allies himself with a people which has been freed from slavery. His law is meant to preserve this freedom.

The law is given in two stages. First, the whole people hears the Ten Commandments as the direct voice of God. It is terrified at the majesty of this voice. Therefore Moses is to receive the further commandments alone and hand them on to the people. Only after that is the covenant concluded. The laws given by Moses between the Ten Commandments (the Decalogue) and the making of the covenant are known as the Book of the Covenant. Israel is committed to this book. Our text comes from it. As the direct voice of God, the preceding Ten Commandments have a higher status. There follow ordinances for the tabernacle and for worship. They are not quite so important.

One episode after this lawgiving is decisive: the people worships the golden calves. It abrogates the covenant with God. In despair Moses shatters the tables of the law. But now he really gets to know God. Now he may not just hear God's voice, but see his glory from behind. And now this God reveals himself as grace. He tells Moses: 'I will be gracious to whom I will be gracious, and will show mercy on whom I will show mercy' (Ex.33.19). He shows his grace by renewing the covenant and having the tables of the law remade. The narrators wanted to make it clear that on Sinai God enters into a covenant with people who are people that really exist, wayward and unreliable – in short, normal people. It is with them that God wills to put his righteousness into practice, not with imaginary people. So God's law is grace.

Any child can hear that in the Sinai story. But we theologians have only slowly come to understand it. For a long time we have set law against grace, law against gospel. The God of the Old Testament has been regarded as a God of justice and retribution, while the God of the New Testament has been regarded as a God of love and forgiveness.

The text which has been chosen for today can contradict such prejudices. A series of commandments in it is aimed at treating everyone equally in court. These commandments aim at justice. But some go beyond that: they require help for the enemy, support for the poor, and for the alien not to be oppressed. They point in the direction which Jesus indicated radically in his command that we should love our neighbour: love for the enemy, the alien, the poor and the outcast. Here more than justice is called for. Here love and mercy are to be shown. One could almost wish that these commandments stood not only in the Book of the Covenant, but also in the Decalogue. What a good thing it would be if all our children learned: 'You shall help your enemy.' 'You shall not oppress an alien.' 'You shall support the poor.'

The former President of what was once Yugoslavia, M. Panic, recently expressed the wish that the Ten Commandments could be extended. He thought that God had forgotten one commandment, 'You shall not engage in ethnic cleansing.' Panic does not know the Bible well. If he did, he would be shocked and offended. Just as some of us will be offended when I tell you that an ethnic cleansing is announced in the Sinai law. It is not forbidden, or condemned, but promised as something positive. We find it at the end of the Book of the Covenant. Shortly after we have heard 'You shall not oppress an alien', we read: 'I will hand over to you the inhabitants of the land, and you shall drive them out before you. You shall make no covenant with them and their gods. They shall not live in your land ...' (Ex.23.31f.). How are these two statements compatible, on the one hand the commandment not to oppress the aliens in the land and on the other the promise to drive them out?

I could have ignored this problem. It would probably have struck very few people that here kindness to the alien and xenophobia lie side by side. This xenophobic text is not in the programme of our gathering. And who reads these texts at home in context? But when I was preparing this Bible study this ugly problem particularly fascinated me. Certainly I am glad that a social commandment like 'You shall not oppress the alien' stands in the Bible. But it pains me that the Bible at the same time promises that aliens will be driven out. In preparing Bible studies I have sometimes sighed, 'Couldn't those in heaven appoint a commission to reformulate some texts in the Bible?' I would propose to this commission that this section of the Book of the Covenant on ethnic cleansing should be deleted completely.

As I reflected on this, I had a theological fantasy. An angel came to me and said, 'We've already appointed a commission in heaven. It is considering a proposal. If you like you can attend the sessions of the commission. First of all the representatives of the proposers will explain their proposal. Then the commission will hear three expert opinions: one from an expert on comparative law in the ancient Near East, a second from an expert on biblical social history, and finally a third from an expert on theological exegesis. After that a decision has to be taken.'

So in my imagination I see the heavenly law commission. Two angels present the proposal. They say: 'Those on earth who have mandated us ask us to state that the commandment not to oppress aliens requires too much of us human beings. We human beings want to live in an environment in which we feel confirmed, in which people are like us, in which they speak and think as we do. Deviation and otherness offends us. Security comes only through the proximity of people whose mere existence signals without words, 'You're normal. You're like us.' When material opportunities are scarce, we band together with like-minded people to impose our interests at the expense of those who are different. And if we're unsuccessful in this, then our hatred mounts against everything that is different. Then there is burning and killing. That is reality. And things have always been like that. So as the commandment about aliens in the Book of the Covenant asks too much, we propose a correction. A very brief addition should be made to the commandment about aliens, which significantly already stands at the end of the Book of the Covenant. The new biblical text should read:

"You shall not oppress an alien. You know what happens to aliens, since you too were aliens in the land of Egypt. To spare others this fate, no aliens shall live in your land and be admitted to it."

The reason for this is that if no more aliens enter the land, the commandment about aliens can continue fully in force without doing any damage. The advantage of this change is that the formulation in the Book of the Covenant remains intact.

When these two angels had finished, there was a disturbance among the angels. A heckler called out, 'Cynicism!' But the president called for order. First it was necessary to form a judgment on what the Book of the Covenant really meant. So he called the first expert, the angel Hammurabi-el, whose speciality was the comparative history of ancient Near Eastern law. He was to make clear what was special about the Book of the Covenant by comparison with other collections of law, above all how the commandment on aliens related to the notion of expulsion.

Hammurabi-el began like a real scholar. He announced that he would sum up the special features of the Book of the Covenant and in addition the law of ancient Israel in three points.

1. All codices of law in the ancient Near East were promulgated by kings. By contrast, Israel attributed its law to God, and that law applied independently of the state. So it could even survive the collapse of the state which Israel had experienced after the destruction of Jerusalem and the deportation of the upper class of Judah. Thus the law could limit the power of the state: for example, the law of the king in what we call Deuteronomy seeks to prevent the king from exalting himself over his brothers (cf. Deut.17.14-20).

2. Israelite law comprises legal, ethical and religious commandments at the same time. A legal commandment – in other words a 'law' – must be legally enforceable. The violation of ethical commandments provokes only contempt from other people, but one cannot enforce their observance by courts of law. The command to go to the aid of one's enemy's donkey if

it collapses is an ethical commandment. No one is prosecuted and condemned for not obeying it. The command about strangers is an ethical commandment. And it is particularly in these ethical commandments that God comes into play: though transgressors may avoid human courts, they do not avoid God. This characteristic juxtaposition of law and ethics leads to the need constantly to reinterpret the law in the light of ethical principles. Israel's law is therefore a law in process of development. Different collections of laws from different stages of development have been preserved side by side in the Old Testament: the earliest is the Book of the Covenant; then follows Deuteronomy and finally the Holiness Code. Thus even contradictory elements come to stand side by side.

3. The whole of the ancient Near East recognizes the obligation of the king and the powerful to take the side of the weak, especially widows and orphans. The special characteristic of Israel is that it imposes this obligation on the whole people. In Egypt the whole people experience what it is to be one of the oppressed and those without rights. Therefore an appeal is made to the whole people to protect the oppressed and those without rights. The whole people takes the role of kings. The whole people is to be a 'kingdom of priests' (Ex.19.6) – that is what is said at the beginning of the Sinai narrative. The circle of the oppressed and those without rights is similarly extended. It comprises not only widows and orphans, who are mentioned all over the Near East, but also aliens. The commandment about aliens is inculcated twice in the Book of the Covenant: the first time in Ex.22.21, where widows and orphans are mentioned alongside aliens, and once again in this passage. No other commandment apart from this is repeated in the Book of the Covenant. Moses knew why he did that: it is particularly easy to sin against this commandment. People would like to limit ethical and legal norms to the native population. This extension of the commandments beyond the circle of Israelites can also be found in later collections of law. The climax of this development is the Holiness Code. It contains the command to love one's neighbour, in Lev.19.18.

And this commandment is explicitly extended to aliens: 'When an alien resides with you in your land, you shall not oppress the alien. The alien who resides with you shall be to you as the citizen among you; you shall love the alien as yourself; for you were aliens in the land of Egypt: I am the Lord your God' (Lev.19.33ff.).

Hammurabi-el now goes on to discuss the important point of how the commandment about aliens and the notion of expelling them relates to the centre of Israelite law. The commandment about aliens is closely connected to the First Commandment – the main commandment for Israel. For that states: 'I am the Lord your God, who brought you out of the land of Egypt, out of the house of slavery; you shall have no other gods before me.' In the Book of the Covenant, reference is made to this first commandment only in the case of the commandment about the alien. Only here is the slavery in Egypt recalled. Because the Israelites lived in Egypt as aliens, they too are now to be fair to aliens. Respect for the alien therefore beyond question derives from the centre of Israelite faith, from the memory of the Exodus from Egypt, from the First Commandment.

But what about the notion of expulsion? Hammurabi-el cannot help us out of this problem. Rather, he emphasizes that his academic knowledge compels him to state that the notion of expulsion in the Book of the Covenant is also closely interwoven with the First Commandment, namely with its continuation: 'You shall have no other gods before me.' The expulsion of aliens from the land is promised because of these alien gods. They are not to remain in the land, 'or they will make you sin against me; for if you worship their gods, it will surely be a snare to you' (Ex.23.33). That is vividly described elsewhere. People come into the land. Their sons and daughters marry those who live there. They bring their gods with them. They issue invitations to their festivals – and already Israel is no longer exclusively worshipping the one and only God. So the land is to be free of aliens, and precisely because of the same commandment which is the foundation for the toleration of aliens.

In conclusion, the commission asks whether Hammurabi-el is arguing for the texts about expulsion to be deleted from the Bible. He shakes his head. Unfortunately one cannot regard the notion of expulsion as a regrettable lapse, as a slip-up in an otherwise lofty ethical tradition. However, as an expert he can point out that expulsions were widespread in the ancient Near East. The Assyrians in particular extended their empire in this inhuman way. Here Israel was not thinking differently from its neighbours. By comparison, the positive commandment about aliens is striking. It seems all the more miraculous, the more one reads it against the background of xenophobic texts in the Bible. But this contradiction remains a riddle.

Hammurabi-el's remarks have provided much food for thought. The commission needs further information. The second expert is called. He is Soci-el, a specialist in biblical social history. He is to explain in what situation this contradictory combination of a high social morality towards aliens and fantasies about expulsion came into being in Israel. Soci-el, too, sums up his thought in three points.

1. The whole Sinai narrative is a protest against the worship of the golden calf. This narrative seeks to show how God can be worshipped in truth – without cultic images and dancing round the golden calf. True worship consists in social behaviour and worship in the tabernacle. Now the tabernacle stands for the Jerusalem temple. We can provide a good historical context for such a narrative: Israel had been split into a northern and a southern kingdom. In the northern kingdom a golden calf was worshipped in the sanctuaries of Dan and Bethel; in the south the temple of Jerusalem was the central cult place. There were only isolated voices of protest in the northern kingdom. There the prophet Hosea attacked the cult of images. He threatened a catastrophe which would come upon the people. His protest was combined with Amos's protest against social abuses. Amos had prophesied a catastrophe even before Hosea. And in fact it came: in 721 the northern kingdom was conquered by the Assyrians, the upper class was deported and many people were expelled. Alien peoples were settled in the land. Only now was

the criticism of the prophets generally recognized: anti-social behaviour and false worship were the causes of the catastrophe. The dance round the golden calf was Israel's great sin. Only after the fall of the northern kingdom was the Sinai narrative given its present form: the tabernacle, the Jerusalem temple, is set over against the golden calf of the destroyed northern kingdom. Only in Jerusalem is God worshipped rightly. Despite the catastrophe in the north, God gives Israel another chance. He shows himself to be a gracious God, who holds fast to Israel despite its breaking of the covenant. God renews his covenant. God has spared the smaller southern kingdom, and God will stand by this southern kingdom if the remaining Israelites convert to the one and only God and keep his commandments.

2. After the catastrophe in the northern kingdom, reform movements came into being in the southern kingdom. To all appearances, the Assyrians would soon also swallow up the small southern kingdom. But the southern kingdom would hardly have offered resistance had the Israelites there believed that with the new masters, only masters were being exchanged; that it did not matter much who ruled – and by what laws they ruled. So on top of old laws, new laws were developed, laws which in a way quite amazing for the time sought to preserve the social interests of the whole people. The Book of the Covenant is the draft of such a social lawbook. All Israelites are to have the same opportunities in law. The hostilities between them are to be replaced by a pro-social attitude; the poor are to be supported. The threat from outside and this attempt at social renewal belonged together. People in Israel discovered the truth that it is not just military strength which gives a nation the chance of survival but its social cohesion, its loyalty to basic commandments for solidarity, its obedience to God's commandment. In any case, in military terms the southern kingdom was hopelessly inferior to the Assyrians, the greatest military power of the ancient Near East. But it was superior by virtue of its legal order and its moral traditions. This produced the singular combination of religious, legal and ethical norms that we find in the Book of the Covenant. Turning to the one God (i.e. the

renunciation of idolatry and the worship of images) was as much a reaction to the catastrophe in the north as were the just laws and the propagation of a social morality which went even beyond the laws.

3. This situation also explains the contradiction between the social commandment about the alien and the fantasies about expulsion. After the end of the northern kingdom many people fled from the north to the south – not only Israelites but also their neighbours, who had similarly been subjugated by the Assyrians. The wave of refugees made the problem of aliens acute. A reaction to this was expressed in an amazing social commandment about aliens, which actually occurs twice in the Book of the Covenant. It was clear that if no help was offered to people fleeing from the Assyrians, the resistance against the Assyrians would be weakened from within. Many Israelites would be abandoned, and along with them many non-Israelite refugees. At the same time fantasies about expulsion were rooted in this situation. The Assyrians had driven out or deported many people in the northern kingdom and replaced them by settling alien peoples. Of course people in the southern kingdom dreamed of finding the land free of conquerors once again. Of course they dreamed of taking possession of the land again. The fantasies of expulsion in the Book of the Covenant are anti-fantasies. They are directed against the cruelty of the Assyrian expulsions and deportations. So the expulsions of which the Book of the Covenant dreams take quite a different form from the Assyrian expulsions: there will be no bloodshed and war. God himself promises that: if his commandments are kept (including the commandments which protect the poor, the weak, and the aliens), then God will drive out the enemies of Israel – simply by his terror and by hornets, but not all at once, or in a year. Rather, what the text says literally is, 'I will drive them out before you quite gradually.' When the Book of the Covenant recalls the expulsion of the original inhabitants, it really means the conquerors in the north. People wanted to get rid of them again – but peacefully, in contrast to the methods of Assyrian military conquest.

From all this Soci-el draws almost a philosophical conclusion. The great solidarity of a community often arises as an
answer to demands from outside. To the present day, humankind lives by the creative power of two small peoples who had
been threatened by far superior military powers: the Greeks and
Israel. The experiment of Athenian democracy came into being
as a response to the Persian challenge. The vision of a social
community based on solidarity came into being in Israel as a
response to the threat from the great powers of the ancient
Near East. In both we keep finding sharp disparagement of
enemies: the contempt for the barbarians among the Greeks
and hostile fantasies against the Gentiles in Israel. Here Israel
had the harder time; the Greeks prevailed against the Persians.
For a long time they belonged to the winners in history. Out-
wardly Israel belonged to the losers – yet nevertheless continued
to develop its ethos of mercy. In both cases the new ideas
developed with a dynamic of their own which points beyond
the situation in which they originated. Once the notion of
freedom has been formulated and begun to be put into practice,
once the notion of social mercy has been expressed and finds an
echo – then in the long run it cannot be limited to a group. In
both the Greek and Israelite traditions we find a development
towards the universalization of freedom and mercy. In Greece
the notion became established that not only Greeks but also
barbarians are people destined for freedom. And there was a
similar development in Israel: not only Israelites but all human
beings are neighbours. The demand for mercy applies not only
to Israelites but to all human beings. The beginnings of this
development can already be found in the Book of the Covenant:
the alien and the enemy are included in the network of pro-
social norms.

Finally, the commission puts to Soci-el, too, the question
whether he is arguing that the notion of expulsion should be
deleted from the Book of the Covenant. Soci-el hesitates. He
points out that one would be causing an important historical
source for the background to the social commandment about
the alien to disappear. So he has his doubts. Perhaps a footnote

should be added to the Bible. However, he would prefer to limit himself to understanding these fantasies about expulsion and explaining them historically without moral condemnation of a past time. Of course he personally rejects such ideas of expulsion completely. He leaves no doubt about that.

The commission has a brief discussion about how it is to proceed further. Its problem is, how can it prevent simple readers of the Bible from justifying their xenophobia by the fantasies about expulsion in the Book of the Covenant? Few readers of the Bible have as much knowledge about it as Hammurabi-el and Soci-el. Is it possible to arrive at a clear repudiation of all forms of xenophobia without such knowledge, simply by taking the words of the Bible seriously – or does one have to criticize the actual content of some texts of the Bible? The angel Exegeti-el, the last expert, is to answer this question.

Exegeti-el gets straight to the point. He says: The conclusion of the Book of the Covenant with its promise of expulsion is indeed problematical. But even if it is taken literally, one cannot read any invitation to expel people out of it. It is not in fact a commandment to human beings but a divine promise. It announces that when the Israelites settle in the land, God will free it for them in a miraculous way. Here we have a specific list of the six peoples who are affected by the expulsions: Amorites, Hittites, Pheresites, Canaanites, Hivites and Jebusites. It is not permissible to include other peoples in this list. For the promise clearly relates only to the settlement, i.e. to the once-for-all process of the entrance of Israel into the promised land.

In contrast to this, the social commandment about aliens is a commandment for all times. It is not limited to a unique situation. If we take the text literally, we must understand it as follows: when Israel has entered the land, from then on the commandment to tolerate aliens in the land and treat them fairly applies for ever.

Nevertheless a great problem remains. The same God who commands people to tolerate aliens at the same time announces that he himself will not tolerate alien peoples in his land. Someone could very quickly make this announcement of God's action a model for human action. So we must be quite clear on some points.

How quickly we overlook the qualifications in this text! The expulsion is to proceed peacefully – even if we ask ourselves whether psychological warfare using panic and biological warfare using hornets is not just as bad as the direct use of force. But even more importantly, the reason given for the expulsion is the danger that Israel could fall away from God through contact with the aliens, that it could betray the sole worship of its God. So it would make no sense to drive out monotheists from the land with an appeal to such fantasies of expulsion. Neither Christian Crusaders in the Middle Ages nor nationalistic Israelis today had or have the right to be inspired by such texts to drive Arabs from the land. Muslims are monotheists. They never lead anyone to apostatize from the one and only God. By contrast, in the ancient world Israel was the only monotheistic people. With its faith in the one God it diverged from all others.

Nevertheless, Exegeti-el finds such considerations macabre. For they could suggest that ethnic cleansings are not intrinsically reprehensible, but only under certain conditions: if God himself carries them out, if they take place with a minimum of force, and so on. So he states quite emphatically: we cannot on the one hand formulate an ethical commandment that people should be tolerant towards aliens, and on the other hand accept religious intolerance without contradiction, e.g. perpetuate an image of God which has xenophobic features. It is precisely this tension that we find in the Book of the Covenant: a tension between the ethical duty to treat aliens well and the xenophobic religious promises. All attempts to interpret away this contradiction are in vain. It points to the future. In later texts of the Old Testament it is resolved. There the fantasies of expulsion are replaced by their opposite: the alien people will not one day be driven out of Palestine, but they will flock to Zion because there is a human justice there which is kind to men and women. Already in the Old Testament God develops into a God of all human beings. We must follow this line of development in expounding the Bible. In the light of it some texts have to be criticized. That is the only way of taking the whole Bible seriously.

The crucial substantive question is: how can we understand belief in one and the only God in such a way that proximity to people of another faith is not experienced as a threat – as something which offends us, with our own convictions, or alienates us from them? Is that possible without our secretly recognizing alien gods (alien words and convictions)? Is tolerance possible without violating the First Commandment – the commandment 'You shall have no other gods than me?'

Exegeti-el now gets to his most important point. Before the Book of the Covenant come the Ten Commandments, with the First Commandment at their head. This is formulated on Sinai in such a way that it can be the foundation for tolerance. But one has to listen closely and note everything that is said in it. I can hardly believe my ears when in fact it actually criticizes Luther's Lesser Catechism. There we have a terrible abbreviation of the First Commandment: 'I am the Lord your God. You shall have no other gods but me.' This version mentions only the repudiation of other gods. Anyone who repudiates other gods is always in danger of also repudiating the people for whom these gods have some value. But two further thoughts are bound up with the First Commandment, which remove this danger. And it is precisely these two thoughts which are absent from Luther's Lesser Catechism.

First the statement, 'I am the Lord your God who brought you out of the land of Egypt, out of the house of slavery.' The one and only God wills to be worshipped only as a God of liberation. He repudiates all other forms of worship. He repudiates all other gods because they do not free. Belief in the one and only God can easily be abused. For example, it can be said: 'God has created everything, done everything. So you must accept everything.' Indeed that is God's will. But this God's will is to be respected only as the will of a God who liberates from

25

slavery. God does not want people to accept everything. God does not agree with slavery. God does not agree with aliens being treated in the way that Israel was treated in Egypt. Only as a liberating power does God call for exclusive worship. Any God who does not lead people to freedom is an idol – even if this is the biblical God. Any God who is used to oppress aliens is an idol. So it is highly dubious that many people learn the First Commandment without the statement, 'I am the Lord your God, who brought you out of the land of Egypt, out of the house of slavery.'

It is equally bad that many people do not know the prohibition against images which is closely connected with the First Commandment. It is absent from Luther's Catechism. It runs: 'You shall not make for yourself an idol, whether in the form of anything that is in heaven above, or that is on the earth beneath, or that is in the water under the earth. You shall not bow down to them and worship them.' Here it becomes clear what idolatry consists of. Here we can see what is being repudiated with the commandment, 'You shall not serve other gods': worshipping the picture of God that we make for ourselves. And precisely for that reason there is a proviso about all our talk of God: God is different. God is far more than our images of him. God is also far more than the images that Christian theology develops of him. God is far more than the images that Jews, Christians, Muslims, Hindus and Buddhists make of him. God is not identical with any of our images of God. And for that reason not all images of God are equally valid or convincing in the same way. Some images of God are much more convincing than others. So those who take the prohibition of images seriously do not think that all images of God and all religions are of equal value. But they assume that other religions, too, have approached the truth in a convincing way and think that they can learn from them.

Only when we are really convinced that we can find something of the truth in the firmly-held beliefs of aliens – even something of the truth about God – does the real reason for fantasies of expulsion disappear. It is not enough to utter moral exhortations that we should be kind to aliens. We must examine all our religious convictions – including our understanding of God – in this connection: do they lead to fantasies of expulsion, strategies for demarcation – or to a love of neighbour which includes the alien?

Exegeti-el has finished his speech. The commission is impressed. In all it has been offered four proposals.

The first proposal had no chance in heaven. So it was tacitly withdrawn by the proposers. They explained what moved them to withdraw it. They had underestimated people. In the breaks during the session they had taken a look at earth. And in many cities they had seen torchlight processions demonstrating on behalf of aliens in the land. There was a particularly large one in Munich. With shame they had to concede that people's shabbiness was not as great as they had thought. Even if it is not without risk, the simple commandment 'You shall not oppress the alien in your land' can be trusted. Without any additions, with no ifs and buts. With no alteration to the constitution in the Book of the Covenant.

Then came the second proposal: a proposal to expand the Ten Commandments in Luther's Lesser Catechism. Children should not just learn that we must not worship other gods. They should also learn why we must not worship them. They should learn why any religious belief always becomes idolatry if it does not lead to freedom, and does not distinguish between images of God and God himself. Moreover this would bring Lutherans and Reformed rather closer together. For the Heidelberg Catechism contains the Ten Commandments without any abbreviation. To my amazement this proposal was accepted unanimously. I had always believed that Lutherans had a clear majority in heaven.

Finally someone also formulated as a third proposal my suggestion that the texts about expulsion should be deleted from the Bible completely and that a commission should be formed to investigate other passages which needed to be struck out. Again I was surprised. The proposal was rejected. The reasons given are interesting.

1. In the Bible it should be clear to anyone that the commandments are not addressed to angels but to people who really exist – to people who are afraid of enemies and aliens, to people who have shabby fantasies of expulsion. If these occur even in Holy Scripture, it may perhaps be easier for some people to take responsibility for them. And once that happens, it is easier to revise them.

2. Christianity is not a religion of the letter but one of the Spirit. Certainly the first Christians loved their Bible, the Old Testament. But they did not recognize everything in it *a priori* as valid. They made a critical assessment of it. They repudiated some commandments. They drew a distinction between the letter that kills and the spirit that brings life. Fantasies about expulsion kill, but respect for the alien creates life.

3. The danger of abuse cannot be excluded in the best of texts. However, God gave human beings not only the Bible but also understanding, the ability to read them critically. The whole tendency of the Bible is clear: every human being is the image of God. God draws no distinction between the native population and aliens, the high and the low, the educated and the uneducated. God is the God of all human beings. Read in the light of this conviction, some biblical texts can clearly be criticized, including the texts about expulsion.

4. The longing for an ethically cleansed text of the Bible is understandable. We all want to live in traditions of which we are unreservedly proud. One can be proud of the Bible. But it contains texts which have to be criticized. It would not be a good thing for those reading the Bible to suggest that everything in the Bible is morally good, that they had to or were allowed to put it all into practice, that they could accept it all. That would lull our own consciences to sleep, dull our responsibility for what we personally affirm and what we do not. In short, all the arguments were in favour of leaving the text as we read it now.

A fourth proposal was neither rejected nor accepted. It was adjourned, and I mention it only for the sake of completeness. It aimed at leaving the Bible as it is (with a few notes on passages which are problematical). What was more important was a short appendix: a selection of texts from other religions to which Christians could say yes. This small collection of texts would document that faith in the God of the Bible calls for respect for other religions. As I have said, this project was postponed. The heavenly commission agreed that it was a project for the next millennium.

This Bible study was given in Munich on 10 June 1993 at the Kirchentag of the Evangelical Church in Germany. Shortly beforehand, a reformulation of Article 16 of the Basic Law had been passed, in fact undermining the right of aliens to political asylum by a whole series of additional regulations. Those mainly responsible for the reformulation underestimated popular reaction; they were surprised at the torchlight processions in cities, involving many thousands of people – 300,000 in Munich alone, who were protesting against arson attacks on the hostels for those seeking asylum.

M. Panic was president of former Yugoslavia for the last six months of 1992. At that time above all Serbs, but also their opponents, Croats and Muslim Bosnians, attempted to create territorially coherent and ethnically homogeneous states by 'ethnic cleansing' in a cruel civil war. The historical and theological remarks on the Book of the Covenant and the Sinai pericope are largely based on F.Crüsemann, *The Torah*, Edinburgh 1996.

The Working of the Holy Spirit in Judaism

The Old Testament Pentecost story

(Numbers 11.1-35)

Now when the people complained in the hearing of the Lord about their misfortunes, the Lord heard it and his anger was kindled. Then the fire of the Lord burned against them, and consumed some outlying parts of the camp. But the people cried out to Moses; and Moses prayed to the Lord, and the fire abated. So that place was called Taberah [i.e. burning place], because the fire of the Lord burned against them.

The rabble among them had a strong craving; and the Israelites also wept again, and said, 'If only we had meat to eat! We remember the fish we used to eat in Egypt for nothing, the cucumbers, the melons, the leeks, the onions, and the garlic; but now our strength is dried up, and there is nothing at all but this manner to look at.' Now the manna was like coriander seed, and its colour was like the colour of gum resin. The people went around and gathered it, ground it in mills or beat it in mortars, then boiled it in pots and made cakes of it; and the taste of it was like the taste of cakes baked with oil. When the dew fell on the camp in the night, the manna would fall with it.

Moses heard the people weeping throughout their families, all at the entrances of their tents. Then the Lord became very angry, and Moses was displeased. So Moses said to the Lord, 'Why have you treated your servant so badly? Why have I not found favour in your sight, that you lay the burden of all this people on me? Did I conceive all this people? Did I give birth to them, that you should say to me, "Carry them in your bosom, as a nurse carries a sucking child", to the land that you promised on oath to their ancestors? Where am I to get meat to give to all this people? For they come weeping to me and say, "Give us meat to eat!" I am not able to carry all this people alone, for they are too heavy for me. If this is the way you are going to treat me, put me to death at once – if I have found favour in your sight – and do not let me see my misery.'

So the Lord said to Moses, 'Gather for me seventy of the elders of Israel, whom you know to be the elders of the people and officers over them; bring them to the tent of meeting, and have them take their place there with you. I will come down and talk with you there; and I will take some of the spirit that is on you and put it on them; and they shall bear the burden of the people along with you so that you will not bear it all by yourself. And say to the people: Consecrate yourselves for tomorrow, and you shall eat meat; for you have wailed in the hearing of the Lord, saying, "If only we had meat to eat! Surely it was better for us in Egypt." Therefore the Lord will give you meat, and you shall eat. You shall eat not only one day, or two days, or five days, or ten days, or twenty days, but for a whole month – until it comes out of your nostrils and becomes loathsome to you – because you have rejected the Lord who is among you, and have wailed before him, saying, "Why did we ever leave Egypt?"' But Moses said, 'The people I am with number six hundred thousand on foot; and you say, "I will give them meat, that they may eat for a whole month"! Are there enough flocks and herds to slaughter for them? Are there enough fish in the sea to catch for them?' The Lord said to Moses, 'Is the Lord's power limited? Now you shall see whether my word will come true for you or not.'

So Moses went out and told the people the words of the Lord; and he gathered seventy elders of the people, and placed them all around the tent. Then the Lord came down in the cloud and spoke to him, and took some of the spirit that was on him and put it on the seventy elders; and when the spirit rested upon them, they prophesied. But they did not do so again. Two men remained in the camp, one named Eldad and the other named Medad, and the spirit rested on them; they were among those registered, but they had not gone out to the tent, and so they prophesied in the camp. And a young man ran and told Moses, 'Eldad and Medad are prophesying in the camp.' And Joshua son of Nun, the assistant of Moses, one of his chosen men, said, 'My lord Moses, stop them!' But Moses *said to him, 'Are you jealous for my sake? Would that all the Lord's people were prophets, and that the Lord would put his spirit on them!' And Moses and the leaders of Israel returned to the camp. Then a wind went out from the Lord, and it brought quails from the sea and let them fall beside the camp, about a day's journey on this side and a day's journey on the other side, all around the camp, about two cubits deep on the ground. So the people worked all that day and night and all the next day, gathering the quails; the least anyone gathered was ten homers; and they spread them out for themselves all around the camp. But while the meat was still between their teeth, before it was consumed, the anger of the Lord was kindled against the people, and the Lord struck the people with a very great plague. So that place was called 'the Graves of Craving', because there they buried the people who had the craving. From the Graves of Craving the people went on to Hazeroth, and remained in Hazeroth.*

Numbers 11 is the Pentecost story of the Old Testament. It tells of the outpouring of the Holy Spirit in Israel, of its activity in Judaism. In so doing it contradicts age-old theological prejudices. For the first Christians regarded the possession of the Spirit as what distinguished them from all other Jews. They said, 'John the Baptist baptized with water. We, and only we, are baptized by the Spirit – no one else.' So the Pentecost story became the story of the foundation of the Christian community, which derived its existence from the working of the Spirit.

We can object to this contrast between Christianity and Judaism with the help of Numbers 11. Numbers 11 is the foundation story of the post-exilic Jewish community, which here is similarly deriving itself from the activity of the Spirit. It tells of the origin of the Sanhedrin, the governing body of the Jewish community. The Sanhedrin consisted of seventy people, in addition to whom there was the high priest as president, just as in our story in addition to the seventy elders there is Moses as supreme authority. Our story does not just seek to relate how and why this body came into being. It seeks to explain why the Sanhedrin is to be respected. It seeks to show that the authority of this body derives from Moses, indeed from God himself. God gave the spirit of Moses to the seventy. And this 'spirit' is the spirit of God.

Both foundation stories, the Old Testament and the New Testament Pentecost stories, show that the Spirit blows where it wills. The Spirit is not a special possession of Christians, but is also at work in Judaism. And in Judaism, too, it blows where it wills; there, too, it does not allow itself to be limited to a particular body. There, too, it seizes outsiders. There, too, it overcomes the limits of institutions and traditions. That is the point.

Before we look more closely at this foundation story of Judaism, here is some information about the institution which stands at its centre, the Sanhedrin.

The Sanhedrin came into being after the collapse of the monarchy, after the return from the Babylonian exile. The Jews who had returned had to give themselves a new constitution. There may have been dreams of restoring the monarchy. But another constitution came to be established: an aristocracy under the leadership of the high priest.

Who belonged to the Sanhedrin? And what competence did it have?

Soon after the exile, 'priests' and 'elders' already appear in the sources as leading groups in Jewish society (e.g. Neh.2.16). But the rise of a third group, the scribes, proved decisive. This rise is closely connected with a special characteristic of post-exilic religion: at that time Judaism founded itself afresh on the basis of scripture. The five books of Moses were compiled. They contained the Torah – God's revelation. Scripture became the supreme authority. All the experts in scripture, the scribes, profited from this. The authority of scripture passed over to them. Thus to the two earlier aristocratic groups – the priestly and lay aristocracy – was added a new educated aristocracy. It was included in the Sanhedrin at the latest in the second and first centuries BCE. So in the New Testament we meet three groups in the Sanhedrin: high priests, elders and scribes. The newest group survived all the rest. With the destruction of the temple in 70 CE, the priests lost their functions and the property-owners their property. But the scribes continued to possess their scripture and refounded Judaism on that basis. They gave it the form that it still has. They understood themselves as the successors of the seventy, to whom the spirit of Moses had passed. So we can say that Numbers 11 is the foundation story of Judaism.

And what competence did the Sanhedrin have? It advised the high priest on religious and political questions, determined the calendar of festivals, and sat as the supreme court. It imposed the death penalty. However, in the time of Jesus the Romans ruled Palestine and reserved for themselves the right to condemn people to death. So it is quite improbable that Jesus was condemned to death by the Sanhedrin. Probably it just laid charges against him. Pilate pronounced the verdict. He was responsible for the execution of Jesus.

Thus Numbers 11 relates the foundation of an institution which came into being at the earliest in the sixth century BCE and disappeared in its then form in the first century CE. This story cannot be older than the institution for which it seeks to be the foundation, and therefore cannot be older than the sixth century BCE. But it is set at the time of the wandering in the wilderness – more than half a millennium earlier. The foundation of the Sanhedrin was transferred back into this initial and primal period – according to the motto, 'The older the better.' The nearer to Moses, the nearer to God. Such projections back on to distant primal times are typical of foundation stories. But quite apart from that, the story has a series of untypical features. Some of them are subversive; they undermine authority rather than provide a basis for it. I hope to make this clear by turning Numbers 11 into a typical foundation story. In anticipation I should emphasize that if there ever was such a version of our story, we should be glad that it never found a place in the Bible – but only in a Bible study at a Kirchentag.

When Israel was travelling through the wilderness, it fed on manna, a miraculous food, which fell from heaven. But there was one disadvantage: it was always the same food. People kept having the same sweet taste in their mouths, the same lumpy feeling in their stomachs. The Israelites kept muttering. They complained to God, 'It's hard enough worshipping only one God. But eating only one food – that's deadly. No one can stand that. Think of our children! Won't they turn away from you as the one and only God if they only get just one kind of food from you? Remember, the stomach is the way to love, even love of God. How are we to love you if we have no gherkins, no onions, no garlic – and above all no meat like we had in Egypt?'

When Moses heard this, he did not have one of his fearful attacks of holy rage, as at other times, but was seized with deep compassion. Here he recognized a special emergency, a need which one understands only if one is a human being – and which therefore had to be brought before heaven gently. He said to God, 'God, do not despise the complaints of the people. It sounds like ingratitude. We have only just escaped from slavery in Egypt, but we are all already longing to go back – simply because for a few weeks our dreams have been full of gherkins, onions, garlic and meat. We are sighing for them like thirsty people for water. You cannot imagine how helplessly captivated we are with these fantasies of vegetables and meat. We are not pure spirits like your angels in heaven. We are human beings of flesh and blood, with bellies, mouths, tongues and noses. If things go on like this, the whole people will soon sell its right as firstborn among the peoples for a mess of pottage. They are so crazy that they will soon worship not only golden calves but gherkins, onions and garlic. They are addicts: for gherkins, garlic and meat. And you know that even for one individual, fighting an addiction is infinitely difficult. For a whole people it's impossible. So help us to overcome this gherkin and meat crisis!'

And Moses succeeded in persuading God. God said to Moses: 'In my Ten Commandments I only imposed belief in one God on them, not eating one food. So let them have what they want. Tomorrow the field around your camp will be full of meat – enough for one month.'

Moses knew his people and therefore he was deeply afraid. 'O God,' he said, 'that is well meant. But there could be a catastrophe. If we put so much meat without any preparation before a people which is so avid for meat, they will all fall on the meat and each will fight his neighbour for the biggest pieces. There will be murder and killing. And I shall stand there in despair. For in their craze for meat they will not listen to my voice.'

Then God said, 'Gather the seventy elders and the most influential men from all the tribes and station them before the camp early in the morning. They shall distribute the meat fairly.'

And so it happened. No Israelite disputed with his neighbour, but the seventy elders gave to each his own, depending on his needs. And all were content and said, 'From now on we want the seventy elders as our supreme authority. They shall solve our problems. For they are as wise and just as Moses.'

My version of the biblical story has the structure of a typical foundation story. In it, first a problem or an emergency is described, and then a solution. The institution for whose authority a basis is to be given in the story produces a solution with which everyone is content. Here is a second example, by way of illustration. In abbreviated form, the story or myth of the foundation of the Federal Republic of Germany goes like this: 'There was great distress in the post-war period, and then Ludwig Erhard brought the social market economy. That produced the economic miracle. It led to riches and prosperity. So to hell with all those who have anything against the market economy.' I am also telling this 'myth' to make it clear that foundation stories are not just meant to be explanations. They give instructions for action. They seek to define what is desirable and what is not. They legitimate forms of life: in the one instance the market economy, in the other the Sanhedrin.

Precisely for that reason we should pay attention when we find unusual features in the foundation story of the Jewish community. Certainly it provides a basis for authority – but at the same time it raises subversive doubts about this authority. It makes authority a problem. I shall now demonstrate that in detail.

Our story depicts two emergencies. First, there is the collective distress of the people, the crisis over meat and gherkins, and then there is the individual distress of Moses, his crisis over leadership and responsibility.

To begin with, let's look at how the collective distress of the people is overcome. Here the 'spirit of God' becomes a stormy wind. In Hebrew, *ruach* means both spirit and wind. This spirit, as a storm wind, produces quails. In this way it overcomes the distress. In the story as we now have it, this spirit is identical with the 'spirit of Moses' which was transferred to the seventy. So these seventy are involved in removing the distress. However, the blessing which they bring about becomes a curse for many people. 'But while the meat was still between their teeth, before it was consumed, the anger of the Lord was kindled against the people, and the Lord struck the people with a very great plague' (Num.11.33). This can be derived from realistic experiences. If one gives semi-starving people solid food without gradually accustoming them to it, there can be catastrophic consequences – even death. But of course our story wants to say more than that. It wants to say that the appointment of the seventy may have resulted in material success, while the greed stimulated by this prosperity kills. This also casts a shadow over the seventy. Their appointment cuts both ways. It brings both life and death. Just imagine the following conclusion to the foundation story of a modern democracy: '...and when the constitutive assembly had done its work there was a great banquet. Half those present died of unexplained causes ...' This conclusion would be a remarkable commendation for a constitution!

The subversive feature of our foundation story becomes even clearer in the overcoming of the second emergency. Moses despairs of his task. He suffers the distress of anyone in a position of responsibility who has to lead a group through extreme situations. His distress reflects the despair of those small groups faithful to Yahweh in the difficult post-exilic period, when it looked as if it would be impossible to persuade a people which had just escaped destruction to understand themselves as witnesses to the one and only God and his messengers.

Moses despairs in two ways, over the people and over God. Moses despairs, because he identifies with the people's complaint. He understands the human longing for good food.

But Moses also despairs because he identifies with God's commission. He is to lead the people to freedom, and now they long to go back to Egypt.

Moses stands between God and the people. What links him with God isolates him from the people. What links him with the people isolates him from God. He is alone. He is lonely.

The answer to his despair is to transfer his responsibility to many people, to transfer the spirit from him to the seventy. From now on these seventy speak and act with the same authority as Moses. But three reservations are made in relation to their authority. And our text makes that into a major story.

The first reservation. The spirit comes upon the seventy. They appear as prophets. Remarkably, immediately after this we read, 'But they did not do so again' (Num.11.25). They stopped prophesying. This continuation is so unusual that almost all translators make a small change in the Hebrew text. They make *lo yasapu* into *lo yasupu*. The original text says, 'And they did not continue prophesying'; the altered text reads, 'And they did not stop prophesying'. The latter would fit better into a foundation story which supported authority: the seventy receive the spirit and through it become prophets – for ever. They continue their prophetic activity. But the original text says the opposite: the seventy have the spirit of Moses only temporarily. It does not have a permanent effect on them. Certainly the text does not say, 'God deprives of understanding those to whom he gives office (like the seventy)', but it does say, 'God does not give his spirit to those to whom he has given an office in such a way that they have it for all eternity.'

That applies to all institutions. They cannot permanently be filled with the spirit of their founders. The spirit of Moses does not fill all institutions of Judaism permanently, any more than the Spirit of Christ can fill the institutions of Christianity permanently. Nevertheless, Jewish and Christian institutions are necessary. For there is no law which says, 'The spirit of their founders must be lost in them for ever.' It remains latently preserved in them. It comes to life in them time and again.

The second reservation. The spirit seizes not only the seventy elders and officials but also two other Israelites who had remained in the camp, Eldad and Modad. In Judaism, as in Christianity, the spirit blows where it wills – often precisely where it had not been foreseen, among people outside official circles. A fundamental insight can also be derived from that: the spirit to which religious institutions appeal is often more active outside these institutions than in them. And the official institutions need to note precisely that. For at the very moment that the seventy stop speaking prophetically in the spirit of Moses, the spirit comes upon two Israelites who do not belong to the seventy. And it is more intensively and lastingly active in them than among the seventy. For it is not said of Eldad and Modad that they again cease to speak prophetically. On the contrary, they do so so lastingly and strikingly that Joshua wants to put an end to their activity.

We can go on to ask, 'Why does the spirit come upon Eldad and Modad in particular?' The story says of both of them, with apparently no motivation, 'They were with the Kethubim.' That can be translated, 'They were among those written down', i.e. on a list which predestined them for the spirit. But there is no mention of such a list elsewhere. An alternative translation (which I find more illuminating) runs: 'They were at the writings.' We should remember that in the post-exilic period a new educated authority developed alongside the aristocracies of the priests and those with property, namely the 'scribes', who were originally not members of the Sanhedrin, but were included in this body later. The scribes were always 'at the writings', the scriptures; they studied them and interpreted them. Eldad and Modad are the first scribes. Initially they embody only a tiny minority. But the Spirit is permanently with them. They are treated with hostility. Joshua, Moses' successor, wants to put an end to their activity. He appeals to succession and tradition. The position of all traditionalists is endangered if people like the scribes can refer directly to the foundations of an institution or a religion by virtue of their education – and have a basis for criticizing it. Paul was a 'scribe' like this, and so was Luther. Every Protestant theologian dreams of being an Eldad or a Modad.

Finally, *the third reservation*. Moses himself turns against Joshua, his successor, and says, 'Would that all the Lord's people were prophets, and that the Lord would put his spirit on them!' (Num.11.29). Since the whole people is explicitly mentioned, the prophets here include both men and women. That is how Joel prophesied: in the end-time all the people will become prophets, all the sons and daughters of Israel (cf. Joel 3.1ff.). Here we have a dream of the universal prophecy of believers, just as we Protestants dream of the universal priesthood of believers. The prophetic spirit of Moses, which is at work in the seventy and in the two outsiders Eldad and Modad, really aims to fill the whole people. The division between the seventy and the people is only an emergency solution. It is provisional, until all are one day filled with the prophetic spirit. The seventy and seventy-two are acting only as representatives of the whole people, until Jeremiah's prophecy has been fulfilled:

'But this is the covenant that I will make with the house of Israel after those days, says the Lord: I will put my law within them, and I will write it on their hearts; and I will be their God, and they shall be my people. No longer shall they teach one another, or say to each other, "Know the Lord," for they shall all know me, from the least of them to the greatest, says the Lord; for I will forgive their iniquity, and remember their sin no more' (Jer.31.33-34).

According to this prophecy there is no longer a division between those who know God's will and the others who have to be instructed in it. According to this prophecy, one day all will know God's will directly.

I distinguished earlier between two emergencies: the collective distress of the people, the crisis over meat and gherkins, and the individual distress of Moses, the crisis of the isolated individual bearing responsibility between people and God.

Now we can see how the narrator who has interwoven the stories of the two crises perhaps imagined their inner connection. Moses wishes that all had the spirit – that there was no longer any opposition between prophets and people, teachers and taught, Moses and Israel. Had his wish been fulfilled, then the unexpected meat mountain in front of the camp could not have had such catastrophic consequences. Had prophetic responsibility been alive in all, then no one would have eaten themselves to death out of sheer greed. Had all been filled with the spirit of Moses, then the solitude of Moses would finally have been overcome.

I hope that I have shown that the story of the foundation of the post-exilic Jewish community emanates an anti-authoritarian spirit through and through. The authority of the seventy is legitimized, but at the same time made a problem. It also has negative consequences. The prophetic spirit does not always work in the seventy. But it keeps appearing time and again in small minorities – and it should really be alive in the whole people.

The image of post-exilic Judaism which follows from this contradicts the picture that my teachers were still giving me when I was a student in the 1960s. There the end of the true prophetic spirit was dated to the foundation of the post-exilic community. Even worse, the new Jewish community that was in process of formation was often described as 'slavery under the law', as an authoritarian culture in which the prophetic spirit that was renewed through Jesus had dawned like an anti-authoritarian rebellion. Now I know that this picture is a caricature of the Judaism of that time. Numbers 11 shows that the anti-authoritarian prophetic spirit continued to remain alive in it. There is no unbridgeable opposition between Moses (i.e. the law), the prophets and the scribes. In Numbers 11 post-exilic Judaism says, rather, that Moses himself was a prophet. He defends prophecy against his successors. One cannot play the law that is attributed to him, the Torah, off against the prophets. So one cannot play off the new Christian experience of the prophetic spirit against Judaism either. That brings us back to our starting point, a comparison between the Pentecost story as a foundation story of the Christian community and Numbers 11 as a foundation story of the Jewish community.

The presupposition of such a comparison is that we read the Old Testament not only as a scripture of Christians but at the same time as a book of the Jews. (I continue to use this term 'Old Testament'; in a society with so many 'old' people there is nothing discriminatory about the adjective 'old'.) For too long the Old Testament has been naively understood only as a pointer to the New Testament. In this sense it was possible to read Numbers 11 as an anticipatory account of Pentecost. But historical-critical research has taught us to see the texts of the Old Testament as important in their own right – quite independently of their relationship to the New Testament. And respect for Judaism, along with a repudiation of the centuries of contempt for and persecution of Jews by Christians, has taught us also to value and read these scriptures as witnesses to another religion. If we do this, we gain a great deal: every time we refer to the Old Testament and refrain from commandeering it immediately as a Christian scripture, we enter into a dialogue with Judaism. The dialogue with this other religion has a place in the foundations of Christianity, and is already given with our Bible, which is in two parts. If we want a Christianity orientated on the Bible, that necessarily follows.

So it would not be a good thing to read Numbers 11 solely as an anticipation of the Pentecost story, as a still incomplete intimation of the working of the Holy Spirit. Beyond doubt there are agreements and analogies. In both cases God's activity is depicted as fire and a stormy wind. In both cases God's spirit seizes people, beyond all social barriers. In both cases the working of the spirit has material consequences: in the former the stilling of hunger for meat, in the latter the way in which the first Christians shared their possessions.

But Numbers 11 has an importance of its own. This story is

more critical and more realistic than the Pentecost story. It is the basis of authorities and institutions, but at the same time indicates what reservations about them are necessary. It depicts the ambivalence of religious institutions, and also their helplessness in the face of vital forces. People obsessed with fantasies of meat and gherkins are incapable of higher things. It gives us a realistic picture of spiritual responsibility, of the despair of those who have been given by God the task of leadership through the wilderness of life into the freedom of God – and who come to grief on the trivial wishes of the average person, who has something different in mind. It is precisely because of this realism that the story has a consoling aspect: God's spirit is at work here, not among imaginary people, but among people who really exist – among people who are consumed by the desire for material possessions, among people who threaten to collapse under the authority with which they are burdened. It also works in the official institutions – but at the same time announces itself in critical minorities.

I want to end by presenting the message of our text in the form of a fantasy. I imagine Eldad and Modad sitting in heaven, studying the internal constitution of present-day Protestantism.

Eldad says to Modad: 'What a remarkable lot these Protestants are! Where two or three of them get together, they form a critical minority. There is no majority, only minorities. Everyone lives in the awareness of deviating from what the majority do. They are all prophets: prophets of human rights, prophets of peace, prophets of ecology, prophets of Israel, prophets of liberation, Third World prophets, muesli prophets. Above all the women prophets are on the increase at present.

Modad: 'But they must also have a Sanhedrin to be responsible for the whole organization.'

Eldad: 'They call their Sanhedrins "church assemblies". These are responsible for the whole organization. Otherwise no one feels responsible. So these church assemblies feel that they are an especially isolated minority, which finds it difficult to make clear to most people what the issues are. However, this minority acts only with restrained Protestant prophetic gestures.'

Modad: 'But sometimes these Protestants do meet as a majority – in Protestant mass demonstrations.'

Eldad: 'You mean the Kirchentags. Then more than 100,000 Protestants assemble – who are at the same time 100,000 minorities. A splendid feeling unites them all: the collective minority feeling. That does them good.'

Modad: 'We shouldn't grudge them that. All of them together form only a small group in their society, with views which are increasingly diverging from the views of society as a whole and with problems which increasingly differ from the problems of most people. In their society many people are choking on their meat mountains, many are perishing because of too high a cholesterol level, because they cannot tame their desire for meat. And then along come these Protestant muesli and wholemeal prophets and preach not only muesli and wholemeal bread, but even worse, food coming from heaven. They preach that human beings do not live by bread alone, but by the word of God. And what do their contemporaries say? "We know that already. We've had that for centuries. It's boring. Always the same thing. God and love, love and God, creation and life, life and creation! I don't want any prophets in this society." People are dying inside, dying spiritually, because most of them are uninterested in what is being said. Or regard it as outdated nonsense.'

Eldad: 'They shouldn't complain like that. They should be glad about the universal prophecy among them. However, there's one thing that they have to learn: democratization of the spirit of Moses also means democratization of Moses' despair. Universal prophecy also means that the depression of the prophets is universal – despair about being isolated between God and human beings.'

Modad: 'Nevertheless, this Protestant fluctuation between prophetic pathos and depression worries me. In Israel very few were prophets – who tormented themselves with God's problems as representatives of the people. But that often spared the others the torment.'

Eldad: 'Was it really only the prophets who knew this torment? Didn't all Israel become prophets? Have these Protestants nothing to learn from us Jews? We Jews bore witness to the one and only God, although that put us in a radical minority role. We endured that for many centuries. We endured it when our own children, these Christians, thought that they had to overtake us. When they looked down on us with pride and contempt because we remained true to our supposedly outdated views. They discriminated against us, persecuted us and killed us because of these views. Nevertheless, as a small minority we have borne witness to the world about our truth. The Protestants are in a far more comfortable situation. They cannot compare themselves with us. They have it far easier that we had it for centuries. They will learn that those who are seized by the prophetic spirit become a minority – and it is a great task to remain faithful to one's task as a minority. Just as Moses remained true to his task, although he often despaired on the journey through the wilderness.'

Now back from heaven to earth, where we can perhaps draw a conclusion from the story of Eldad and Modad: the prophetic spirit certainly does not work only in Christianity. It also works in Judaism. It works there far more convincingly than it does among us. if we recognize that, despite all that has happened we can enter into a new dialogue with Judaism. Only one thing is required of us as a presupposition: the readiness to learn from Judaism. And the readiness to reckon with the working of the spirit in its traditions and institutions.

In our story the Sanhedrin is attributed to this spirit. But someone could now say, 'Didn't this Sanhedrin later hand Jesus over to the Romans? Doesn't that disrupt all attempts to build bridges between Jews and Christians with the help of the experience of the spirit?' No! On the contrary, the Sanhedrin is *a priori* seen in a critical light in the story of its institution. The spirit of Moses is not always with its seventy members. The spirit can also seize people outside this circle, people whom

Joshua and other successors of Moses would much prefer to suppress forcibly – contrary to the will of Moses. At that time they were called Eldad and Modad. Later they were called Jesus and Paul. All four are Jews. Judaism *a priori* included in the report of the foundation of its leading body an indication that this body is not infallible. It would have been good had Christian authorities and institutions always been aware that they, too, are not infallible.

This Bible study was given at Bochum on 7 June 1991, at the Kirchentag of the German Evangelical Church in the Ruhr, and on 13 October 1991 in Versailles.

Seduction to Life

A women's story from a male perspective

(The Book of Ruth)

(The text of the Book of Ruth is too long to be printed here. It can be found in the Bible between the books of Judges *and* I Samuel*)*

Why do we find the story of Ruth and Naomi so attractive? One answer could be that this story undermines prejudices in a gentle way – prejudices between peoples, between poor and rich, between man and woman. We also find such prejudices in our religious traditions. Unfortunately we cannot say that they are just absurd misunderstandings. We keep coming across them even in the Bible. Here are three examples.

First a prejudice against other peoples, against foreigners. In the Bible we read: 'No Ammonite or Moabite shall be admitted to the assembly of the Lord' (Deut.23.3). In other words, foreigners are not wanted. Foreigners are excluded. But the Book of Ruth tells of a foreign woman who was accepted into the assembly of the Lord. It tells of a Moabite woman who converts to the Jewish faith.

The second example is the prejudice which attributes poverty to human failure. It is not easy to find an example of this in the Bible. As a rule the Bible contradicts such judgments. But once it, too, says, 'For the drunkard and the glutton will come to poverty' (Prov.23.21). However, the Book of Ruth tells of women who neither drink nor guzzle, yet find themselves undeservedly in distress.

A third example relates to the relationship between man and woman. The Bible tells how after the exile Ezra enforces the dissolution of all mixed marriages between Israelites and foreign women (Ezra 9.1ff.). By contrast the Book of Ruth tells demonstratively of a mixed marriage between the Israelite Boaz and the Moabite woman Ruth.

So the book tells of a foreign woman, a poor woman and a wife. Each role, that of foreigner, poor woman and wife – especially a widowed and childless wife – in itself represents a social setback, and this is even more the case with the combination of all three roles. Yet these setbacks are overcome. All the prejudices which get in the way of a human relationship between native born and foreigner, rich and poor, man and woman, are subversively undermined, and without any great drama. How is that possible?

The first answer is: through faith in the God of Israel. This faith breaks through social barriers.

The second answer is: through human loyalty, especially the loyalty between two women of different peoples.

The third answer says: through eroticism. It appears in this story as a seduction to humanity. A seduction scene brings about the decisive turning-point.

In my view, the attraction of the story of Ruth lies in this combination of religious faith, human loyalty and eroticism. It's a marvellous story. It's almost too beautiful to be true. It's good to find such fictions in the Bible.

I want to imagine that this story was already being told in the lifetime of Boaz and Ruth in their home town of Bethlehem. Boaz was praised for marrying poor Ruth; Ruth, for standing loyally by her mother-in-law when all had forsaken her. Of course in doing this the inhabitants of Bethlehem put them in an ever more favourable light. On every re-telling the story became more beautiful, the characters more human, their motives more humane. The truth disappeared behind the poetry of sheer humanity. Only one person still knew the truth, old

Boaz himself. But he didn't tell anyone. The truth lived on only in his conversations with himself, where a person is alone with God, where one can acknowledge even unpleasant truths which one does not want to acknowledge to anyone else. Just suppose that we could listen in on old Boaz talking to himself. Granted, that would be rather indiscreet. But we might perhaps allow ourselves to do so if we bridled the moral desire to condemn and required just one thing of ourselves, to be as fair to Boaz as we are to ourselves. No one is a saint.

So Boaz is talking in an inner dialogue to himself, and some-times also to Ruth and to God. This is what he says.

It all began with a famine. Ehimelech, my cousin, got into difficulties. That story has often been told, but what is not said is that it was the duty of our clan to support Ehimelech and his family. We were all suffering under the famine, though he was suffering more than we were. We could have helped. We didn't.

In emergencies everyone is his own neighbour. Ehimelech emigrated to Moab with his wife Naomi and his two sons. I can still hear him saying bitterly in the village, 'People in Moab aren't so hard-hearted as they are here.' He meant us, his clan. We were the hard-hearted ones. We had failed. When it was already too late I went to Ehimelech's closest relative, a first cousin. I won't mention his name; it deserves to be forgotten. So I shall simply call him the 'caring cousin', as he had an obligation to intervene. Anyway, I urged the caring cousin to help Ehimelech. I promised him my support. But he would have none of it. 'Let them go to Moab,' he said, 'let them believe that the Moabites are better people than we are! Let them believe this nonsense! Do you know what Moabites do in emergencies? They slaughter their firstborn sons for their God Chemosh, to atone to him. That's how philanthropic they are. We don't sacrifice any human beings! We sacrifice no one. So he wants to go to these killers. He'll come crawling back. We can still help him then.'

Ehimelech emigrated, with his wife and two sons. The sons married in Moab. Ruth became his daughter-in-law. Everything seemed to be going well. But then death struck. The sons died. Ehimelech died. All the men died, leaving three childless widows, three women with no social security. Naomi wanted to return to her homeland. She had male relations there – the only protection for an old widow. Ruth followed her; the other Moabite woman left her. She remained in Moab. She had protection there from male relatives. But you, Ruth, chose the more difficult way, the way abroad. You didn't want to leave an old woman in the lurch.

When you appeared again in our village there was intolerable gossip. The people of Bethlehem said, 'Naomi went away rich, and she's come back poor. God has punished her for seeking refuge with Chemosh, the God of the Moabites who kills children. He took her children from her. He caused both her sons to die. He made her daughters-in-law childless. She has entered the realm of the dead. The curse of the God of Israel lies upon her.' Today no one wants to be reminded that they all talked like this. On the contrary, they all claim that it was Naomi herself who said, 'I went away full, but the Lord has brought me back empty' (cf. Ruth 1.21). So everything has been turned upside down.

But I don't want to condemn anyone. I joined in this foolish talk. Why did I do it? I know the reason now: I had a bad conscience. But I didn't have the courage to acknowledge it. Then the simplest solution was to put the blame for their misfortunes on my poor relations. It was not we who had failed; no, God had punished them. We were not the ones who had left them in the lurch, but God had cast them out. O God, forgive me for that. I'm now ashamed that I believed this nonsense. True, I was only repeating what others had said. But I should have known better. For already then I had doubts. The doubts came when I heard what was said of Ruth.

In the village Naomi told people why Ruth had come with her. She told how Ruth had promised her, 'Where you go, I will go; where you lodge, I will lodge; your people shall be my people, and your God my God. Where you die, I will die' (cf. Ruth 1.16f.). That didn't fit into the picture of Moabites who killed children. You, Ruth, were living proof to the contrary. You were a Moabite woman who refused to sacrifice an old, frail person. You stayed with Naomi, though things would have gone better for you in Moab. You didn't leave her in the lurch, whereas our clan had failed. And so you became the embodiment of my bad conscience.

Our clan wasn't exactly enthusiastic when our poor relations reappeared in the village, and not just because of our guilt-feelings. There were quite tangible considerations. Ehimelech had owned a field which in his absence we had regarded as our property. Every relative hoped finally to acquire it after Ehimelech's family had died out. But now the widow was there. She had a claim to the field. Anyone who wanted to acquire it had to provide for the widow. That was no problem in itself. Had Naomi come by herself, our caring cousin would have acquired the field for a ridiculous price – with the promise to support Naomi. As Naomi was already old and near death, there was a foreseeable end to this obligation to support her. But now Ruth was also there. Ruth was young. Ruth didn't seem likely to die soon. Perhaps she would marry and then make claims on the field for her son. So someone would have paid for the field without being able to acquire it. Of course our caring cousin tried hard not to have to look after Naomi. And I was no better. I was happy that I was only a second cousin to Ehimelech, whereas our caring cousin was a first cousin. So he had the first option to buying the field and with it the duty to support Naomi. I made that quite clear to him. 'It's your concern now,' I said, 'it's not on to leave a member of the clan once again without help.' Indeed I threatened to bring the case before the court of elders. That sounds caring. But in reality I only wanted to put him in front of me, so that I wasn't in line. God, who knows our hearts, knows that I didn't have the social conscience I appear to have in the official story. I was just as concerned as our caring cousin to get out of having to care for poor relatives.

How confused I was when I met Ruth for the first time at the harvesting! Ruth, you met me as a poor women, not as a relative. You were gleaning in my fields, gathering the ears of corn that the harvesters had dropped. That's the right of the poor among us. Really we should have left some ears of corn unharvested in the corner of the field. They are for the poor. But who does that now? None of our fields seemed to have any corners, not even mine! But I did leave you the ears. For me your turning up was like a slap in the face. It demonstrated to the whole world that we didn't care for our relatives. If I had treated any poor person as I treated you, I would have offended against an unwritten law. And you could have confronted me with not only the law about the poor but also the law about relatives. Inwardly at that time I resented you: why didn't you go into the fields of our caring cousin? After all, he was responsible for you. Why did you come to me? Why me?

I attempted to make the best of the situation. First of all I saw that Ruth wasn't driven away by the harvesters, as happened elsewhere, even on my fields. Otherwise I didn't intervene. But then I saw to it that a few ears were left for Ruth. I allowed her to drink the water we had brought with us, and invited her to share in our lunch. The public was to see that I was not as shabby as our caring cousin. Above all I wanted to prevent Ruth from going to other fields the next day. What a disgrace that would have been for our clan! The whole village world have pointed a finger at us: 'This rich clan allows its relatives to beg and even sends them to other people's fields.' Perhaps Ruth didn't notice all this. As a foreigner she was not yet familiar with our customs and legal traditions. Perhaps she regarded me as someone with average social attitudes. Dear Ruth, I was certainly not that.

And then there is something else which so far I haven't mentioned to anyone; indeed I'm still embarrassed to talk about it. In Israel we have a legal tradition which obliges us to marry the widow of a brother who has died without children and have a child by her. This child is then regarded as the child of the dead brother. That prevents the clan from dying out, and the heritage can be kept together. This institution (levirate marriage) is a purely social one. It has nothing to do with personal attraction to the widow. It's her social security. Now there were no brothers. But it was in keeping with this tradition for cousins, too, to marry widows. I detected a secret expectation that for social reasons I should marry old Naomi, and I found that distasteful. I knew that I was doing Naomi a bitter wrong. And that's why I'm so embarrassed. But I was oppressed by the thought of having to marry an old, worn-out, embittered wife who could reproach me for the rest of her life: 'Why did you leave us in the lurch during the famine?' and I would have to ... No, I didn't want to do that with her. All that severely burdened my heart. At night I often woke up terrified. I had the feeling that someone was lying on me – an old woman. Of course that was nonsense. In reality it was Lilith, the demon who occasionally visits us men by night, provokes confused fantasies and brings death. Such fantasies are quite normal. But somehow I was ashamed because of these obscene images in me.

I much preferred to see Ruth. I saw her every day during the harvesting. Every day I let her glean, and gave her yet more corn. I enjoyed her gratitude. I was delighted when the harvesters spoke well of her. I was content to be regarded as caring again. The negative image of our clan had been demolished. And as the harvest was good, I was in a good mood. I was in a good mood generally. Until it became clear to me why. I enjoyed seeing Ruth. You, Ruth, were no longer a poor relation. To me you were a wonderful woman, a young woman. Your image haunted me. And I needed your image. The terrifying ghost of old Lilith vanished when I thought of you. You became my anti-Lilith. I was sad to see the end of harvesting approaching, and with it the time when I met you every day. Would you still be interested in me after that? I was already old. There were more attractive young men in the village. The mood in the village had shifted in favour of Ruth. Everyone saw how she was looking after Naomi. Everyone praised her loyalty. Everyone liked her. All the signs were that one of our young men would marry her. But this thought was bitter to me. For in the meantime I had fallen in love with Ruth. For me Ruth was youth and life, while

Naomi was death and dying.

The end of the harvest came, and with it the turning point.
Old Naomi sent you to me when I was sleeping on the threshing
floor after threshing and winnowing. 'Wash and anoint yourself,' she had said, 'and put on your best clothes and go down
to the threshing floor. Wait until he is asleep. Then go and
uncover his feet and lie down; and he will tell you what to do'
(cf. Ruth 3.3f.). That was an invitation to seduction. It's very
innocent to interpret the advice of old Naomi otherwise.
(Though it should be noted that this innocence is widespread in
exegetical commentaries.) And so the inevitable happened.
When I had gone to sleep on the threshing floor that night, I
had another nightmare. Lilith was crouching on my chest. She
took my breath away, put her arms around me. I was filled with
panic. I shouted out in the night. However, it was not Lilith
lying beside me but you, my anti-Lilith. That was my salvation,
more beautiful than any dream. I enjoyed lying by you, feeling
your presence with my body. This simple nearness was more
tender than any tenderness.

But things did not turn out as Naomi had predicted. She had
said, 'Boaz will tell you what to do.' But I was speechless. I
couldn't say anything. I didn't tell you what to do, you told me
what to do. 'Spread your cloak over your servant, for you are
the redeemer – for me and Naomi' (cf. Ruth 3.9).

That was crazily ambiguous: here was a young woman
offering to sleep with me – in exchange for caring for an old
woman. I was angry. However, I wasn't angry at Ruth or
Naomi, but at myself. Finally I had let things go so far that both
women had to put themselves in this ambiguous position. We,
your kinsfolk, had led them to engage in this seduction. We had
driven them to prostitute themselves. And I was entangled in it.
I wanted to make amends. I didn't want to exploit the dependence of this woman. So I said to Ruth, 'May you be blessed of
the Lord, my daughter; this last sign of your love for Naomi is
even finer than the first, your decision to accompany her to her
native land. I will not abuse your trust. I will do everything
possible to buy your field. I will look after Naomi – and win

you as a wife. You could easily find a rich man to marry you. You could easily look after yourself. But you also want to make sure that Naomi is looked after. That is what makes you so loveable.'

God, you know what happened after that. But you also know that I promised her marriage before things went any further.

And because I was concerned about Ruth's marriage, I sent her home before dawn, so that no one should learn about our night on the threshing floor. And I gave her as much barley as she could carry in her cloak, for herself and Naomi.

I secretly asked Naomi for forgiveness that in my fantasies she had become a monster – the demon Lilith. Without Ruth she might perhaps have become a witch in our village. Just imagine if she had returned without Ruth, in a village where many people had done her wrong. We would have read our bad consciences into her – and vilified her as a witch. Perhaps one day I would really have said, 'She's a demon. She is in league with Lilith. She is Lilith herself.' And if anyone had fallen sick in the village, people would have gossiped, 'the witch is responsible for that'. If anything had caught fire, people would have whispered, 'That was the witch.' Then it would have been no use pointing out that belief in witches is forbidden in Israel. Belief in witches and demons keeps cropping up. But Ruth saw to it that Naomi was accepted among us again – not as a poor old thing struck by God, not as a case for social welfare, but as a member of our clan. Ruth's love for Naomi achieved all that.

Now I had to overcome another obstacle. I had threatened our caring cousin that I would bring him before the court of elders to make him finally accept his social obligation to care for Naomi. But now I had to persuade him definitively to renounce this duty of caring and cede it to me – in a legally binding form and as soon as possible. Of course I could have married Ruth as things were. Then our caring cousin would have redeemed the field – the duty of caring for Ruth would have lain with me. And I could also legitimately have spent something on her mother-in-law at no great expense. But the caring cousin would have owned the field, largely relieved of the burden of caring for the two women. So I wanted to have the field unconditionally. That wasn't immoral, but it also wasn't completely disinterested.

The very next day I called the elders together in the gate and also had our caring cousin summoned. I presented the case: 'Naomi wants to sell her field. As next of kin you have the first option to buy it, coupled with the duty to care for Naomi all her life.' 'Now declare,' I went on, 'whether you are claiming your prior right, since I come only after you. If you renounced your right, I would be prepared to buy the field.'

The reactions of the caring cousin were predictable. 'Far be it from me,' he said, 'to leave Naomi in the lurch. After all, we are a caring clan. Of course I will buy the field.'

I became somewhat unsure. Had our caring cousin perhaps heard something of our rendezvous on the threshing floor? Was he reckoning that I would take care of Ruth by marriage? Now I had to bluff, and act as though I had no personal interest in Ruth. So I added: 'Naomi is prepared to sell the field only if the purchaser also marries Ruth the Moabite woman, at least as a concubine. That is her condition. Otherwise she will not surrender it.'

I saw from my caring cousin's face that I had summed him up rightly. With a red face he said: 'That I cannot do. In that case I would be paying for the field three times. First, today, the purchase price; then the obligation to look after Naomi all her life; and finally, I would have to leave it to Ruth's son without a penny compensation – without the field being part of my heritage. I cannot do that to my children. I would be taking away from them everything I invested in this field. Far be it from me to do that. I renounce my prior right to purchase.'

That was my great moment. I declared that I wanted to acquire the field. So Ruth became my wife.

We soon had a child, Obed. Only now did I get to know Naomi properly. The aura of death vanished from her face. Naomi blossomed again like an almost withered tree in which the sap

is rising one last time, so that blossoms wave on the branches
and the twigs are decked in green. Naomi sat with the child on
her lap as though she were his mother. And she said, 'I was in
the land of death. I was in a foreign land. There I died the death
of the alien, without kinsfolk and without descendants. But
now with Ruth's help I have returned to life. Now things are
bright and clear again. God has returned into my life.'

But soon after that her strength declined. She became weak
and felt the approach of death. Fever shook her old body. Pain
overwhelmed it. Yet she kept having lucid intervals. Ruth
looked after her, wiped the sweat from her brow and fed her
broth. Once Naomi seemed to speak as in a fever, confused but
also wonderful words. Like a poem. Sense seemed mixed up
with nonsense. I can only make an imperfect attempt to set
down what she said. She said something like this, while Ruth
held her hand:

Fall back
into the great hands,
black are the hands,
black as death.
Once we travelled
into the land of death.
Once we came back again.
Who will accompany me now?
Now, to where life comes from?
Will I find refuge there?
I am an alien.
Ruth, stay by me.
Your love is life.
No, stay here, Ruth.
Give me something of your love.
You will carry me,
I am easy to carry,
I am becoming very light
– very small, smaller and smaller,
smaller than Obed.

I am changing back,
back into an embryo.
Who is my mother?
Who is my father?
What is my beginning?
At the beginning the seduction to life.
At the beginning love.
Back to the beginning.
Father,
mother,
mother,
father,
God.
There I shall find refuge,
for ever,
beyond the pain.

So Naomi babbled on. And then she became quieter and quieter. She died peacefully. She emanated a great stillness. It was as if God were holding his breath. We mourned her and buried her.

That's Boaz's story. With it I have attempted to illuminate the biblical story, a story which gently undermines prejudices: religious prejudices, social prejudices, gender-specific prejudices. They are undermined by religious faith, human loyalty and eroticism. This biblical story is really so beautiful that it speaks for itself. But isn't it too beautiful to be true? To end with, I would like to put three thoughtful questions to the story.

Let's begin with the undermining of gender-specific prejudices. It takes place through erotic seduction. But that seems too simple. Being in love is always helpful when it's a matter of changing behaviour and attitudes. It's as if the cards have been reshuffled for the game of life. Possibilities that had been covered over are opened up. How easy this Boaz found it to change for the good! But not every man crouching in the prison of his prejudices is freed from it by a young woman like

Ruth. And how attractive this 'liberation' is for him! Who wouldn't do good if he were seduced to it by a young woman? But in that case is he still doing good for the sake of the good? A moral purism can take offence at this. But that's what real life is like: the good often only has a chance when it is combined with strong interests. These create neither the new person nor the new man. But perhaps it is not so reprehensible to move the old man to do good. Nevertheless, some dissatisfaction remains.

That brings us to the second point: the story undermines social boundaries, the boundaries between peoples, between the native population and aliens, rich and poor. But it also sheds a searching light on these boundaries: one misses in it any outcry against a world which offers two women only humiliating methods of securing their right to life, beggary and prostitution. Certainly Boaz prevents extreme humiliation. He turns alms into presents. He first promises marriage and social protection for the women on that memorable night – and only then do the couple remain together until dawn. But precisely this shows that the two women are dependent on such an encounter, which they cannot compel and enforce. Their vulnerability is clear precisely from the way in which Boaz mitigates it. What is the use of a happy ending in a world with humiliating economic dependencies, in which women are driven to the verge of prostitution – if this world remains unchanged? At least it has to be said that the two women do not just appeal to the social conscience of the rich Boaz. They also appeal to the traditions of Israelite law. They appeal to the right of the poor to keep the gleanings. They appeal to the right of relatives to be 'redeemed' by their clan. They want more than grace; they want their right to life.

Yet one last problem needs to be addressed. This story is about the overcoming of religious prejudices. Someone could say that the prejudices we have to undermine today are greater than those in the story of Ruth. Ruth converts to the God of Naomi and Boaz. She shares the faith of the land into which she has come. In this way she is no longer an alien but a native. But today the challenge is that of living alongside people who do not share our faith, who do not convert, people who not only do not share our religious faith (which indeed many of our compatriots do not), but to whom many of the basic values on which our society is based are alien. Should the acceptance of others, aliens, be made dependent on the degree to which they share our convictions?

So in conclusion, one more look at the story of Ruth – against the background of these modern problems. Our question is: to which God does Ruth convert? What understanding of God do we find in this story? How is it related to the understanding of God in the Bible generally? In other words, what is Ruth deciding when she says to Naomi, 'Your God is my God?'

She is deciding to help the last representative of a family condemned to extinction, to remain with her until she dies. She says, 'Where you die, I will die – there will I be buried.' And by this decision she achieves the improbable: the family does not die out but lives on. She becomes the bearer of a great hope. Later the story was told that Ruth became the ancestor of David and the Messiah. New life emerges from a family doomed to death: salvation for Israel – and for all peoples.

This is no chance feature. The first mention of Israel in world history is on the victory stele of Pharaoh Merneptah from the year 1220 BCE. There the Pharaoh boasts after a successful campaign in Palestine that among others he has conquered a people called 'Israel'. What he actually had chiselled on the stele was: 'Israel has no seed.'

Israel has no more descendants. In his view Israel is condemned to extinction. It has always impressed me deeply that the first mention of Israel in world history outside the Bible is a mention of annihilation. But God begins a new history specifically with this group exposed to annihilation – with those who have escaped from Pharaoh. The group threatened with extinction becomes the vehicle of new life, not for its own descendants, but for all men and women.

This is the God whom Ruth confesses. Her confession does not just consist in the words, 'Your God is my God.' Even more, her confession consists in her actions: she makes life possible for those who seemed condemned to extinction, for the weak who had no opportunities. She acts in the spirit of this God, who led Israel out of the slavery of Egypt, who gives a new chance to those threatened with annihilation.

If we already judge aliens by their values and convictions, we should also judge them by the way in which they act.

Let us measure them by the criterion which Ruth's behaviour gives us. Let us measure them by the way in which they support the weaker members of their families. I am certain that we will often be taught lessons by them. Ruth's family solidarity is often far more marked among foreigners than it is among those of us who live in our homelands. By contrast, we usually behave like the clan of Boaz. We behave like the anonymous 'caring cousin'. We all too readily avoid the most obvious solidarity – with both the members of our family and whole groups.

In conclusion, a dream which the story of Ruth led me to have. I dreamed that the story of Ruth was happening among us again. That a new Ruth is living among us unrecognized, somewhere in Germany. Perhaps she comes from Yugoslavia. Perhaps she comes from Turkey or Poland or some other country. Perhaps she is escaping civil war, hunger or poverty to begin a new life among us. Granted, among us she could not become the mother or grandmother of a new 'king', as Ruth became the ancestor of king David in Israel. For we no longer live in a monarchy; we are a democracy. But why shouldn't she be the mother of a future Federal Chancellor? I have to confess that since I had this dream, whenever I hear our present Chancellor talking on the television about foreigners and those seeking asylum and hear his well-meant words, this dream becomes a real longing! Why?

This Bible study was given to the Munich Kirchentag of the Evangelical Church in Germany on 12 June 1993. Here are some explanations.

According to II Kings 3, the Moabite king Mesha in great tribulation sacrificed his son. He was besieged in the city of Kir-

Haraseth by Israelites and Edomites. An attempt to break out failed: 'Then he took his firstborn son who was to succeed him, and offered him as a burnt offering on the wall. And great wrath came upon Israel, so they withdrew from him and returned to their own land' (II Kings 3.27). The Mesha stele depicts the clash between Moabites and Israelites from the Moabite perspective. See the text and commentary in D.Winton Thomas (ed.), *Documents from Old Testament Times*, Nelson 1958, 195-200. The demon Lilith is mentioned in Isa.34.14. She is identical with the female Babylonian storm demon *lilitu*. Because of the affinity of her name with the Hebrew *laylah* (= night) she was understood to be a nocturnal ghost. A translation of the Israel stele of Merneptah (1219 or 1220 BCE) can also be found in Winton Thomas, 137-42. Some scholars understand the statement 'Israel has no seed' literally: because of the devastations Israel is threatened with a famine, in which the seedcorn for the next year will be eaten up.

The Transformation of
Complaints and Laments into
a Confession of Guilt

(Psalm 51.1-15)

Have mercy on me, O God,
according to your steadfast love;
according to your abundant mercy
blot out my transgressions.
Wash me thoroughly from my iniquity,
and cleanse me from my sin.
For I know my transgressions,
and my sin is ever before me.
Against you, you alone, have I sinned,
and done what is evil in your sight,
so that you are justified in your sentence
and blameless when you pass judgment.
Indeed, I was born guilty,
a sinner when my mother conceived me.
You desire truth in the inward being;
therefore teach me wisdom in my secret heart.
Purge me with hyssop, and I shall be clean;
wash me, and I shall be whiter than snow.
Let me hear joy and gladness;
let the bones that you have crushed rejoice.
Hide your face from my sins,
and blot out all my iniquities.
Create in me a clean heart, O God,
and put a new and right spirit within me.
Do not cast me away from your presence,
and do not take your holy spirit from me.
Restore to me the joy of your salvation,
and sustain in me a willing spirit.

Ash Wednesday is a day and a symbol: the beginning of Lent and a symbol for the great disillusionment, when all masks fall. This year there was no carnival, but the masks nevertheless fell.

The mask fell from our politics. We believed that we had despised war as a political means. We were convinced that our politicians would refrain from waging wars as long as there were other means. But it proved that although there were other means, war was risked, chosen and willed with cool calculations.

The mask fell from our society. We are proud of our freedom. But we have exchanged this freedom for dependence on oil. We are dependent on oil as on drugs, ready to get our supplies by any means, including criminal means.

The mask has fallen from our economy. After the collapse of the planned economy it resonated in our consciousness for a year that we had the best of all economies. Commenting on the East, an expert said, 'The attempt to organize the economy in accordance with ethical principles failed.' Socialism was this attempt. So is capitalism an attempt to organize the economy in accordance with immoral principles? At least this year it proved that the economy functions extremely well on the basis of amoral principles. Countries were armed to a tremendous degree out of a desire for profit. For the sake of profit our engineers kept building rockets until they threatened Israel – and with Israel also our moral integrity.

More masks will fall, masks behind which a cruel war is hiding, masks of censorship, masks of propaganda. How terrible this war must be, that even Western democracies have to hide its cruelty! Our politicians know all too well that if we all really knew the terror and inhumanity of a night of bombs in Baghdad or Tel Aviv, a cry of dismay would paralyse them. They would soon no longer be able to wage war.

When the masks fall, there is great caterwauling. Christians have the task of turning this caterwauling into a confession of sin, so that we can say with the psalmist,

For I know my transgressions,

and my sin is ever before me.
Against you, you alone, have I sinned,
and done what is evil in your sight.

Why is it so important to transform moral caterwauling into a confession of sin, in other words into the consciousness of having transgressed against God? The decisive difference between the two is that caterwauling is moral paralysis, and the consciousness of sin is moral pain.

Caterwauling is paralysis as a result of disillusionment. When we tear off all the masks from civilized people, so that their brutality and savageness comes to light, then we always arrive at the same result: human beings have always been brutal and savage, they still are, and will continue to be so. We cannot change that. We shall not change that. That is how it is.

By contrast, consciousness of sin is moral pain. Pain is indispensable for life. It makes it possible for the organism to react to dangers. It makes possible reactions which can save life. It is at the service of life. It is at the service of change. No one can survive without feeling pain.

Sin is moral pain. Those who stifle the consciousness of sin in themselves, stifle the signals which lead them to change their behaviour. All attempts to dispel the consciousness of sin by therapy, regarding it as an exaggerated false reaction, fail to recognize this. Of course there is such a thing as a neurotic consciousness of sin. Anxiety is important for life. But too much anxiety can be a neurotic phobia. Order is important for life. But too much of a compulsion for order can be a neurotic obsession. A consciousness of guilt is important for life. But an excessive consciousness of guilt can destroy life through depressions. Precisely for that reason, we must not want to remove anxiety and order or guilt. That would be like wanting to stifle a sense of pain that is important for life. This is a feeling which perhaps torments us and is a burden, but which makes us ask, 'What else can we do?'

The awareness of sin is moral pain which is always focussed only on one point, on God. 'Against you alone have I sinned.'

You alone – the God who is the creator of all life.

If we transform caterwauling into an awareness of sin before God, we will achieve two things. First, where there is sin, forgiveness is also possible. Then we can say with the psalmist,

> *Have mercy on me, O God,*
> *according to your steadfast love;*
> *according to your abundant mercy*
> *blot out my transgressions.*
> *Wash me thoroughly from my iniquity,*
> *and cleanse me from my sin.*

Caterwauling can never be forgiven. Only sin can be forgiven. Secondly, where there is sin, change is possible. Then we can say with the psalmist,

> *Create in me a clean heart, O God,*
> *and put a new and right spirit within me.*
> *Do not cast me away from your presence,*
> *and do not take your holy spirit from me.*

Caterwauling does not create a clean heart, a right spirit which looks to the future with new confidence.

Today, on Ash Wednesday, the masks fall. But they are not all that falls today. One could call the whole modern world a global Ash Wednesday, a chain of disenchantments and disillusionments. Our culture is a culture of caterwauling, and we have excellent control over our cultural technology: we can wail quite stirringly in a routine way, and always hit some mark.

But if we present everything to God, we must put off one last mask behind which we often hide in order not to become vulnerable – the mask of our disillusionment, our cynicism, our unbelief, which says that human beings will always remain the old predators, superficially domesticated.

When we go before God, we acknowledge that God has made us in his image. Not as predatory animals. Not as bomb-throwers. Not as military strategists. God has made us as human beings to whom he has given responsibility for their life and his creation. God trusts that we will live up to this responsibility. God will asks us, 'What have you done with your life and my creation?'

Then we cannot bring our caterwauling before him and say, 'We've waged wars. People have always done that and always will do that. Pity.'

'We've made ourselves as dependent on oil and other material possessions as on drugs. And that won't change. Pity.'

'We've earned money in the arms trade and by exporting death. Everyone does. Pity.'

'We've swept the abomination of war under the carpet, so that people don't get too disturbed. Pity.'

And then God will say, 'You cynics! Couldn't you say at least once, "We did that wrong", "That hurt", "That was a crime against God and human beings"?' Dear people, I cannot give an answer to what we have done wrong as individuals. I can only make suggestions about how we might act otherwise. And we shall discuss such suggestions together. But I do know one thing.

If we say that war is sin – and we cannot avoid doing so – then we have a great promise. War is not a natural event that comes upon us. It comes from us. Wars do not happen. Wars are waged by people. The key to them lies with us. We must look for it in ourselves. We may often fail on the way to a world in which war is finally despised. But we may constantly look forward to the overcoming of war. We may constantly pray,

Have mercy on me, O God,
according to your steadfast love;
according to your abundant mercy
blot out my transgressions.
Wash me thoroughly from my iniquity,
and cleanse me from my sin.

Amen.

Traces of Light

A sermon at the Wednesday morning service, 13 February 1991. The Gulf War had broken out precisely four weeks previously, in the night of 16/17 January 1991. News blackouts spread the fear that we were not being fully informed about the terrors of the war. After the collapse of Communist rule in Eastern Europe the leading German sociologist and social philosopher N.Luhmann put forward the thesis that the failure of the centralist state economy showed that in principle the economy could not be guided by ethical principles. The Gulf War seemed to confirm this thesis in a quite different way from that intended by Luhmann: Iraq had been highly armed for the sake of profit – not least by German firms, but also by other Western countries. Now these weapons were being turned against Israel and other Middle Eastern countries. The whole situation was an invitation to limit the quest for profit by ethical considerations and to direct it by political means.

Life – A Hymn to God in the Face of Death

(Psalm 118.17-19)

I shall not die, but I shall live, and recount the deeds of the Lord. The Lord has chastized me, but he did not give me over to death. Open to me the gates of righteousness, that I may enter through them and give thanks to the Lord.

That is the language of someone who has escaped once again: escaped a fatal accident, been freed from the suspicion of an incurable illness, acquitted on a serious charge. For anyone who has had this sort of escape, life shines out anew – like light in the darkness, like spring in winter. Such a person rejoices. God has kept his word.

But that is only one side of the matter. When Diogenes saw the numerous thanksgiving inscriptions in the temple of Samothrace – inscriptions put up by those who had been saved from shipwreck – he remarked, 'And how many more there could be had all those who drowned in the sea been able to hang up their thanksgiving inscriptions here!' What are we to say to this comment by the Cynic philosopher? I have two answers for Diogenes.

My first is, 'He's right.' Indeed, he was far more right than he thought. For one day we shall all belong among the drowned. The hour will strike for all of us. The time will come for all of us when 'I shall not die' will no longer be true. For each of us one day it will be 'I am dying' – even if we have escaped with our lives a hundred times previously. It is one of the great graces of life that the dead take the knowledge of their last torment with them to the grave. Perhaps that is the only way in which those of us who are alive can go on living in our innocence.

But I have a second answer for Diogenes. How many more thanksgiving inscriptions would hang in Samothrace if all the living perpetuated their thanksgiving there in writing? Doesn't each one of us have thousands of occasions for gratitude? Doesn't each of us have reason to give thanks for being here today – for having irrefutably lived to the present day? For having got up this morning, for breathing and seeing the light?

Will our gratitude be refuted by being confronted with the twilight before death?

No, I keep telling myself. This twilight, which will come upon me as it will come upon everyone else, is perhaps only the dark counterpart to the great hymn to life – just as deeper pangs of love are the price of great love. We sing this hymn to life every moment that we exist. We sing it without sound and voice when we see, hear, breathe, smell. We sing it as a hymn to the bond between all things which has brought us into being and which we involuntarily affirm when we affirm our little, vanishing life.

I believe that the whole of life is an unconscious hymn to this life in the most comprehensive sense – to the life of God, in whom our life is hidden. It is a hymn at the abyss of death. And here it is often particularly loud and irresistible. The affirmation of life has never come over me so powerfully as when at the age of eighteen I stood by my brother's coffin. A flood of infinite affirmation of life came upon me between waves of pain and grief. So much was enigmatic. For my brother had been infected by an illness which had passed harmlessly over me. It took him away, but I lived on. I escaped, new born, but at the cost of another life. At that time it seemed to me that for the first time I would live consciously. The mere existence of all things became a great song with a theme on which I could continue to compose variations. Thus even the life of my brother which had suddenly been broken off seemed to find a kind of continuation in my life. Had I known the Bible better at that time, I might perhaps have said, 'I shall not die, but I shall live, and recount the deeds of the Lord.'

But it would not have been possible for me to add, 'The Lord has chastized me, but he did not give me over to death'. 'Chastize' is an old-fashioned word. It means a punishment aimed at educating. Chastizement is a reaction to bad behaviour by pupils and children. But are the crises and catastrophes of life merely consequences of guilt and failure? I do not believe that they are.

But I do believe that all crises and catastrophes are an opportunity to change life. And in this sense I can make my own the image of God as the one who educates us in reality. All the situations in which I experience something contrary, in which I run aground, beach myself, almost perish, possibly contain a message, *the* message: 'You must change your life! Now you have a chance to change it!' If I approach the painful situations of life with this attitude, I can react much more constructively than if I am obsessed with bitterness and resignation. And that applies even when it is clear that one day suffering will prove too much for me and will lead to death. One day life will end. But even then there will be another message: then it will no longer be about overcoming this suffering; it will call on me to endure it, to bear witness to a life which is not contradicted by death.

But where can one get this education? Where is there a school which teaches us to sing praises to life – and in so doing not to leave out the dark counterpart of death? As Christians we have a unique opportunity. We have all stood at the grave of our brother. We can all experience at his grave how all pride in life is crucified and buried. We can all experience that this is not the end of everything. The courage to live of all those who are associated with this brother will rise again – every day. We will be associated with him in life and in death. We will continue a different life in our life, which has died in his place. And between waves of pain and mourning in this life we shall always be caught up in a flood of infinite affirmation of life. And we shall time and again sing and say the great hymn of praise to life itself, to God.

I shall not die, but I shall live, and recount the deeds of the Lord.

And may the peace of God which surpasses all our understanding, keep your hearts and minds in Christ Jesus. Amen.

This sermon was given at a Wednesday morning service in St Peter's Church on 17 April 1991. The anecdote about Diogenes, the famous Cynic philosopher, can be found in Diogenes Laertius, *Lives of the Philosophers* VI, 59: When someone marvelled at the votive offerings in Samothrace, he said, 'How many more there would be if those who had not been rescued had put up their votive offerings here.

Dreams, Stars and the Distinction between False and True Prophecy

(Jeremiah 23.16-29)

Therefore thus says the Lord of hosts: Do not listen to the words of the prophets who prophesy to you; they are deluding you. They speak visions of their own minds, not from the mouth of the Lord. They keep saying to those who despise the word of the Lord, 'It shall be well with you'; and to all who stubbornly follow their own stubborn hearts, they say, 'No calamity shall come upon you.' For who has stood in the council of the Lord so as to see and to hear his word? Who has given heed to his word so as to proclaim it? Look, the storm of the Lord! Wrath has gone forth, a whirling tempest; it will burst upon the head of the wicked. The anger of the Lord will not turn back until he has executed and accomplished the intents of his mind. In the latter days you will understand it clearly. I did not send the prophets, yet they ran; I did not speak to them, yet they prophesied. But if they had stood in my council, then they would have proclaimed my words to my people, and they would have turned them from their evil way, and from the evil of their doings. Am I a God near by, says the Lord, and not a God far off? Who can hide in secret places so that I cannot see them? says the Lord. I have heard what the prophets have said who prophesy lies in my name saying, 'I have dreamed, I have dreamed!' How long? Will the hearts of the prophets ever turn back – those who prophesy lies, and who prophesy the deceit of their own heart? They plan to make my people forget my name by their dreams that they tell one another, just as their ancestors forgot my name for Baal. Let the prophet who has a dream tell the dream, but let the one who has

73

my word speak my word faithfully. What has straw in common with wheat? says the Lord. Is not my word like fire, says the Lord, and like a hammer that breaks a rock in pieces?

On one occasion when I was invited to give a lecture, I was asked not to make it academic, but to speak with prophetic authority. I could understand the antipathy to academic lectures, but the request to play the prophet offended me. No, I said to myself, you're an exegete. You're a preacher. But not a prophet. You have no direct line up there. So I said no. I didn't want to be a false prophet.

But how can one distinguish between true and false prophets? In retrospect that's easy. The humane Marxist prophecy of a just world has dissolved into moralistic caterwauling. The inhumane prophecy of a Third Reich in which one pure race rules over the others collapsed in a catastrophe. The prophets of pure justice and pure race have proved to be false prophets. In retrospect!

But what about today's prophets? What are we say to the sympathetic wholemeal and muesli prophets? Aren't they right? Don't we live by the death of other life when we eat meat? And what are we to say to our ecoprophets? Are the traffic gridlocks on our streets signs of a breakdown of the world's circulation? Ten years ago a student told me, 'In two years we shall all be irradiated.' Did he only get the date wrong? And finally the prophets of peace. Will we survive the collapse of great empires without devastating wars?

Should we listen to these prophets? Or is it better to give up prophecy completely and formulate hypotheses which are open to correction? Scientific hypotheses always contain a prediction, a degenerate form of prophecy, which is confirmed and corrected by experiments. Such hypotheses cover processes which are regular, and which we can repeat and control. But this procedure is successful only in nature. In history everything is unique. Nothing recurs as it was before. Only analogies between the earlier and the later can be discovered in retrospect, and perhaps guessed in anticipation. The future escapes the proven grasp of our reason.

Can we learn from the prophets of Israel here? They transformed the recollection of the past into a model for the future – and were also open to new things. They based their expectations on unique events and allowed themselves to be corrected by history. Could they teach us a rational approach to the future and history? Or do they present a hopelessly obsolete form of coping with the future?

Jeremiah already had this problem. Anyone who argues with false prophets is arguing with two modern forms of coping with the future. At the time both seemed to be more up-to-date than prophecy. Let's give a hearing to two advocates of this new prophecy, and let's call them Astariah and Onariah.

This is what the prophet Astariah says: 'You have heard how Jeremiah fulminates against us. Our bones are to be taken from our tombs and scattered before the sun, moon and the whole host of heaven because we have loved the stars, served them and asked questions of them' (Jer.8.1ff.). Jeremiah is furious because we have imported a well-tried form of prophecy from Babylon and Assyria: the observation of the stars. This marks the beginning of a new era. For the first time scientific judgments are being made about the future. They are being made systematically and on the basis of empirical observations. They make us independent of such irrational ecstatics as Jeremiah. The people who use our methods have been reinforced by their success: the Assyrians and Babylonians have built up empires in the name of the Baal of heaven, the God of the stars. By contrast Israel, with its old-fashioned prophets and men of God, has become dependent on them.' But Jeremiah angrily counters: 'What kind of a moral quagmire have you got yourselves into? You even sacrifice children for your future out of a fascination for your stellar law. You allow children to go through the fire to achieve a divine verdict or to secure your future, or simply to imitate barbaric Assyrian customs. Anyone who sacrifices human beings because he thinks he has insights into the laws of the world and history is a false prophet. He does not speak in the name of the living God. He does not speak in the name of life, but in the name of death.

In the text for our sermon Jeremiah has to cope with another form of prophecy. Let's listen to its representative, the prophet Onariah. He says with all the pathos of ancient Israel:

'Thus says Yahweh, who has always revealed himself though dreams. Think of Jacob, who in a dream saw the heavens opened and became certain of his salvation. In such dreams God reveals himself in primeval images which we may trust. They are more helpful than cool calculations of the future made by the stars. They speak to us. They give us courage – more courage than the depictions of catastrophe by our former prophets. They reconcile our unconscious with our consciousness. They bestow shalom: peace with ourselves, totality and security.'

But here, too, Jeremiah objects: 'You tell the people that all will be well with them. No disaster will come upon them. That is why you get on so well with them. But you're no better than the stellar prophets. They sacrifice children to their terrible reality, but you sacrifice reality to your wishes. You do not dare to confront people with reality. For you do not know that those who transgress against reality are punished by life – often with inexorable harshness, as if the wrath of God were inflamed against them. It should be your duty to deter people from their perverse ways – instead of flattering the unconscious.'

What can we learn from all this about false prophets? First, in the Bible a false prophet is someone who imports an alien value system into Israelite society, who speaks in the name of the Baal of heaven and not in the name of Yahweh. By contrast, the convictions of the true prophets are in solidarity with the people.

Secondly, there are also false prophets among those who speak in the name of Yahweh: they appeal to common values in order to confirm the people in the way that it is taking instead of confronting it with its failure, its dishonesty and its disloyalty to common convictions.

But what is the sign of the true prophet? Among the false

76

prophets, stars and dreams had become a mysterious scripture which was deciphered by a modern knowledge of the future. By contrast Jeremiah referred to the word of God. He credited this word with tremendous force. He makes God say of it, 'Is not my word like fire, and like a hammer that breaks a rock in pieces?' The true prophet therefore does not go by stars and dreams but by the word of God. But what does that mean?

Jeremiah was convinced that a message is hidden in the events of history. It cannot be read off external events. It is heard only when it is seen in connection with God, when it is put in a new light by a profound vision. To do that there is no need to calculate the course of the stars or to descend into the depths of dreams. To do that one needs to pay intensive attention to everything that is happening in reality. Then perhaps one will hear the message, decode its meaning. Then it will not be history that speaks, but God will speak through history.

History does not give meaning, but in a dialogue with God it becomes a vehicle for signs. Even in a secularized world we speak of the 'challenge of the hour', of our 'responsibility for history'. But who is making the challenge? To whom is responsibility shown? Jeremiah was convinced that these are demands of God. God calls for responsibility. God's call can be heard in the challenges of history.

But today don't we have great difficulties with such prophecy? Aren't we uncertain whether we can hear God's call at all? We experience the world as dumb. It seems indifferent to our wishes and complaints. But what if this dumbness is not grounded in the reality around us – if it comes about because our ears are stopped, because we have programmed our brain not to be provoked by this call? Aren't we right to suspect that there could be something that we fail to hear, but that the prophets heard? In that case the question arises: how can we make ourselves more sensitive? How can we become open to this voice?

The Bible is good for that. Two images in our text can help us here, two images which Jeremiah uses for the call of God: the images of fire and the hammer. For he makes God say, 'Is not my word like fire, and like a hammer that breaks a rock in pieces?'

God's word is like fire. Fire initially means destruction. But it is also a word for love. For powerful, blazing, consuming love – the love between Yahweh and Israel as Jeremiah describes it. Yahweh wooed Israel like a beloved in the wilderness. And she could answer with the Song of Solomon:

> 'Set me as a seal upon your heart,
> as a seal upon your arm;
> for love is as strong as death,
> passion fierce as the grave.
> Its flashes are flashes of fire,
> a raging flame' (8.6).

A fire is kindled in those who are called by God. It is as though they were in love. In this state all doubts as to whether life and the world are meaningful have vanished. Life has a centre. Everything that is in contact with this centre is good. To be in the presence of the beloved is happiness in itself. Other people perceive the same beloved, but they cannot understand this effect.

It is precisely the same with those who are encountered by the word of God. They are in love – not, however, with a person, an idea, with this or that, but with life itself – a life of which their own life is merely a weak echo. Faith is a desire for being. Faith is being in love with reality itself. Other people have the same experience but do not hear this. They are all secure in the same power, but it kindles fire only in some of them. They are all called, but only some respond with a confession of love and faith. God is near to all, but only to some does he become the God who is a presence.

In the course of life this love story with God can become a firm bond, a marriage and all that goes with it: searing marital crises, adultery and reconciliation. An eternal covenant. A Yes to it is an unconditional Yes to life. So one thing is clear: it is impossible for anyone who has once been seized by the fire of this love to let children go through the fire. That is an abomination wherever it takes place, whether in ancient Israel or in Sarajevo, or in the townships of Johannesburg, in Boipatong and Tokoza.

That brings us to the second image. God has a dark side, the God who is at a distance. For the word of God is not only a messenger of love; it is a hammer which shatters rocks. It encounters us as annihilation and death. Matthias Claudius saw this death as a powerful hammer. He writes:

'Ah, it is so dark in the chamber of death,
so mournful a sound when he moves,
and now he raises his heavy hammer
and smites the hour.'

Where death strikes in life, we are stunned. Everything becomes still. The dead disappear into a silence beyond our understanding. But we who live on are asked, 'Have you lived in such a way as to have been true to the covenant with life?' 'Or have you been faithless?' 'Have you been adulterers?' 'Have you spoilt life?' And then the call can come to us, 'Repent! You have this life only once! God has given it to you only once. And what have you done with it so far?'

This call also comes to us in historical catastrophes. The dead of Vukovar, of Sarajevo, of Boipatong – they all cry 'Repent!' Life punishes those who do not repent in time. Those who do not hear in catastrophes the call to repent hear only the voice of their dreams and wishes. And they say, 'That sort of thing will not happen to us.' They suppress the realization of how thin the veneer of culture is. It can be scratched at any time, even among us.

So the word of God is both the hammer of fate and the fire of love. God calls from afar and from nearby. True prophecy expresses both an unconditional Yes to life and a clear No to its transgressions. We can also measure our muesli-, eco- and peace prophets by these criteria.

Of course we should take them seriously. However, we

should contradict them if they put themselves in the succession of the stellar prophets who think that they can disclose the future by observing nature and can thus tell us what to do. That's an illusion. A look at the facts alone will never tell us what to do. Any 'should', any orientation on life, is an added value to what is observed. Anyone who thinks that they can calculate this added value accurately and make stringent plans for the future on that basis will soon begin to sacrifice children for it.

But we should also contradict today's prophets when they put themselves in the succession of the dream prophets. As if our wishes and dreams decreed what should be and can be! No, in all that we do we are involved in a harsh controversy with reality – even when we are attempting to discover what we should do and may hope. And we have not created this reality. It is there before us in all its refractoriness.

The prophets of Israel were convinced that any added value to meaning which provides an orientation for the future is not created by us, nor can it be read off the facts of history. It discloses itself to us when we hear the call of God in our history. Then we enter into a dialogue in which everything is open.

Only one thing is certain: there is value, meaning and happiness simply in entering into this dialogue.

Only one thing is certain: we need not read this Yes to life off the world and justify it. That's impossible. The world is much too sorry a place for that.

Only one thing is certain: we need not stubbornly foist this Yes on the world as though we were the ones who made the conditions for it. If we do that we overreach ourselves.

It is certain that we are responding to a great Yes that we have heard before. Borne up by this certainty, we can endure many uncertainties, uncertainties in society. What follows from this Yes to life for the protection of unborn life? Discussion about that is going on in our midst. It is also going on deep within me. I have no prophetic message here except the message that it is our task to endure uncertainty – and that there is no satisfactory solution.

And then there are the uncertainties in our own lives. Sometimes it is a tormentingly long time before we make out our own task, our own direction. Here too I am helped by the question, 'Is it perhaps your task to endure uncertainty, and perhaps even make something productive out of it?' That can also be the message.

If I got another invitation to give a prophetic speech, how would I reply? Perhaps I would write:

Dear people,

I have no more prophetic authority than you. Jeremiah saw a time coming when everyone would be seized by the prophetic spirit. In a great vision he says, to you as well:

> Thus says the Lord,
> I will put my law within you,
> and write it on your heart;
> I will be your God,
> and you will be my people.
> No longer shall some one teach the others,
> instruct his brothers and sisters,
> 'Know the Lord',
> but you will all know me,
> great and small,
> thus says the Lord;
> for I will forgive your guilt
> and your sins I will remember no more (after Jer.31.33-34).

Each of you has the gift to discover what God's will is for you. It is promised to all of you. No one need wait for a prophet. No one depends on instruction from outside. God trusts you to hear, judge, decide and discern for youselves – and that includes discerning between true and false prophets, good and bad lectures, good and bad sermons. Amen.

This sermon was given on 28 June 1992 in St Peter's Church, Heidelberg. For the view of the prophets and especially the prophet Jeremiah which underlies the sermon see K.Koch, *The Prophets*, II, SCM Press 1983, 13-79. The sermon was given shortly after the massacre in Boipatong, in the Republic of South Africa. Forty-one black Africans were murdered in it. The suspicion that elements of the white government were involved in this massacre was justified: evidence mounted that reactionary groups of the white government, the army and the police wanted to demoralize the black majority by terror and compromise their leadership, the African National Congress. At the same time the civil war in Yugoslavia led to the destruction of the city of Vukovar and the expulsion of its Croat population. In Germany the dominant topic was a decision of the Bundestag a few days previously to liberalize the law on abortion.

Blessed are the Poor in Spirit

The First Beatitude between the left and right wings of Protestantism

(Matthew 5.3)

Blessed are the poor in spirit,
for theirs is the kingdom of heaven.
Blessed are those who mourn,
for they will be comforted.
Blessed are the meek,
for they will inherit the earth.
Blessed are those who hunger and thirst for righteousness,
for they will be filled.

What I would like to do most in this sermon is to keep reading these words out to you in a series of variations. For I know that when we meet there are people among us for whom things are not going well – in the midst of many for whom things *are* going well.

I'm thinking of people who feel poor and wretched. Not in money and intelligence, but in the spirit that brings success in life. They often feel as dead as lumps of clay; as Adam must have felt before God breathed his spirit into him – that spirit which first brings life to life. They cannot imagine this life-bringing spirit embracing them, putting them on their feet, helping them to walk upright; they cannot imagine finding a partner in life who is flesh of their flesh, and being happy with that partner.

I'm thinking of those among us who are sad. Saddened by crises and blows of fate. Sad because their life is coming to an end, because they have to prepare for death. Sad because they are lonely. Sad because the unjust distribution of opportunities of life on this earth depresses them. Some are chronically sad – and the attempt to hide their sadness makes them even sadder. Because they, too, want to belong, to belong to the many who live their lives without burdens, in whom there is a balance between tears and laughter, good moods and bad.

I'm thinking of people among us who cannot make their mark. Gentle people, people whom one can't help liking. Because they always think of others first. They want to put things right for everyone. But inwardly they complain, 'Who takes any notice of me?' 'Who thinks of me?' 'Why are the others always engaged in elbowing their way through life?'

I'm thinking of people among us who have been hurt, who have had no justice, who hunger and thirst for recognition.

The First Beatitude applies to them all. It is the heading to all the rest.

Blessed are those who are poor in the spirit which brings life,
poor in the spirit which brings joy,
poor in the strength to make a mark,
poor in the inner strength to overcome hurts.
Blessed are those who lack the spirit
which brings competence in life,
a capacity to do good,
strength to bear the knocks and the blows,
that brings life with it.
They shall receive the spirit of life.

I can only guess how many obstacles this message has to overcome to reach you.

Perhaps I myself am an obstacle. How easy it would be for someone to say, 'You spoke well. All's well with you! You're lucky. Often very lucky.' And I could only say, 'Yes, I've little chance of getting anywhere in the noble contest over who is the unluckiest.'

And the second obstacle. That is looking at others, those among us for whom things are going well. If I look round, I can see many people here whom the psychologists call Yavis people. YAVIS: Young, Attractive, Verbal, Intelligent, Social high level. People who are what we would like to be all our lives. Those for whom things are going very badly can even resent the presence of such lucky people, because they constantly compare themselves with them. Though even such YAVIS people aren't necessarily happy. I found the term in a description of the clientèle of psychoanalysts.

And now to the main obstacle: mistrust of ourselves. Sometimes I think that the creation story needs to be rewritten to explain this mistrust. When God created the human being of clay and inbreathed his spirit, one of the angels was full of envy because the human being had had preferential treatment. So he breathed his envy into the human being. Since then we sometimes hear a voice which whispers to us, 'Don't believe that you're worth anything. Don't believe that you are the image of God. In reality you're only a useless lump of clay, a bit of rubbish. Don't imagine that others love you. They only say a few nice words to you out of compassion for the lump of clay. Don't believe that God loves you. God says so in his word, but it isn't true. God simply cannot concede that his experiment with the lump of clay was a mistake. God is too courteous to tell you to your face that the experiment with you went wrong.'

Against all these voices I want to set the words of Jesus, which say, 'Blessed are you who are poor in spirit, poor in the life-giving spirit.' Jesus says:

> 'Come to me, I will give you my spirit, which gives you confidence in yourself. I will give you my spirit, which makes people who feel like the dregs the image of God. I will give you my spirit, which gives sovereign power over the insults and defeats of life. I will give you my spirit, which turns

sorrow into blessing, mourning into joy; which overcomes your inner paralysis, so that you become capable of doing good and taking steps in the direction of the kingdom of God.'

I said at the beginning that what I would like to do most was simply to keep saying the same thing to you in a series of variations.

But I must defend my understanding of the Beatitudes against objections. I must overcome not only the obstacles which are present in each one of us and which make us mistrust the good words of Jesus. There are also objections to the content of the Beatitudes.

When I was preparing this sermon I had the following fantasy. I was called before two exegetical tribunals which reported to me that there were substantial objections in principle and of other kinds to my understanding of the Beatitudes.

The first exegetical tribunal was a committee of left-wing Protestantism. I immediately recognized many theologians, male and female, who are very close to me. All in pullovers and jeans. This was their accusation.

You are continuing a pernicious tradition with your interpretation of the Beatitudes. You are spiritualizing them.

Why do you say 'Blessed the poor' and not 'Fortunate are the poor'? For this is about happiness, manifest good fortune.

Why do you say 'Blessed are the poor in spirit' and not (like Luke), 'Blessed are the poor, those who are really poor'?

And why do you say, 'Blessed are the poor in Spirit, for theirs is rule in heaven?' When you do that you shift consolation into heaven, away from the earth into a pale beyond. Why don't you simply say, 'Theirs is the rule'? 'The poor rule.' That sounds much better.

I want to parry this with the counter-argument that they have to address their criticism to the evangelist Matthew. For he speaks of 'poor in spirit' instead of 'poor', of the 'rule of heaven' instead of 'rule'.

But then the exegetical ambition to defend Matthew comes

over me. And I say: The poor in spirit in Matthew cannot be played off against the poor in the literal sense. His gospel of the rule of God is concrete. He says that the blind see, the lame walk, lepers are cleansed, the deaf hear, the dead are raised – and the poor have the gospel preached to them. This clearly means poor in a literal sense: but the one who is poor in the literal sense is soon afflicted with poverty in the spirit, that spirit of which Matthew on one occasion says, 'The spirit is willing but the flesh is weak.' This spirit is the will to life. Those are poor in spirit in whom the will to life has been shattered, buried under avalanches of misfortune, including avalanches of concrete distress and poverty, including sorrow at the scandalous conditions on our earth.

Furthermore, there is no reason to criticize the evangelist Matthew for speaking of the kingdom of heaven. He does not speak of it in a spiritualizing way, as if it were happiness in a utopian nowhere. That is clear from the parallel Beatitude about the meek. They are promised the possession of the earth, just as the spiritually poor are promised the possession of the kingdom of heaven. The earth is the place of the kingdom of heaven. Heaven on earth is before the evangelist's eyes. And this heaven on earth begins wherever people who are poor in the power of life regain that power.

But in no way may we criticize Matthew for offering mere consolation. No, he expects us to do something for it. The way to heaven on earth is for him a 'way of righteousness'. And in Matthew righteousness is something that one should do. Many people go along this way of righteousness: John the Baptist, and even the Pharisees and scribes. But the followers of Jesus are to go further on this way. Their righteousness is to be greater than that of the Pharisees and scribes. Their commitment is to surpass them – by concrete acts of love.

Because of this defence of the Gospel of Matthew I am immediately summoned before the second exegetical tribunal: the biblical committee of right-wing Protestantism. This time serious gentlemen sit before me in dark suits, one wearing a gown and a pectoral cross. He is probably a bishop. They address me very courteously.

Unfortunately they have to object to my exegesis because it continues a suspect moralizing tradition. I am said to understand the Beatitudes as a description of Christian life – as Christian ethics – except that I have exchanged the old-fashioned concepts like 'virtue' and 'morality' for competence in life and spirit of life. But my basic mistake is that I understand the Beatitudes as indications of what people must do, what they must achieve, namely attain competence in life.

And then this man in a gown says to me: 'Why don't you keep to the text: "Blessed are the poor in spirit?" The rule of God begins where God pronounces people righteous through his Holy Spirit, where God acts alone, and where human action is excluded. Those are said to be blessed who know that they are radically dependent on God's action, on God's spirit. They are those who expect everything from God and attribute nothing to themselves, those who humbly trust in God. So the Beatitudes are a pure indicative, a promise of divine grace. But your exegesis turns them into an imperative. And the promise of the divine spirit becomes the promise of a renewed human spirit which brings about competence in life.'

Despite such accusations I feel confident. For I know that in this group I have half won if I base myself on scripture, and that cannot always be said of my left-wing Protestant friends. And I know that I have won hands down if I can even quote Luther.

First of all I defend my interpretation of the 'poor in spirit' as referring to those who are poor in the human spirit of life and will to life. I am certain that this passage is about the human spirit and not about the Holy Spirit. For just as later there is praise of those who are pure in heart, so at the beginning there is praise for those who are poor in spirit. We find the same grammatical construction in both passages. Both heart and spirit are to be read and heard in parallel. This is the spirit which governs the human heart, the spirit which is willing where the flesh is weak. The poor in spirit are those among whom the spirit is no longer willing but shattered, bent, broken. The rule of heaven also means that they will come to rule again in their own lives, instead of allowing themselves to be ruled by sorrow, anxiety and a lack of courage.

So the Beatitudes are not an imperative. They seek to open our eyes to something that is already present, something that is already happening.

Let's look at the situation in Matthew. Here the hurt and tormented people flock to Jesus: 'all the sick, those who were afflicted with various diseases and pains, demoniacs, epileptics and paralytics, and he cured them.' Then he goes up into the mountain, and while the people are standing in the background he says to his disciples, 'Blessed are the poor in spirit – those who are poor in life-giving spirit.' That's an invitation to the disciples: look at this crowd of desperate people whom Jesus has helped! Look at these homeless people! There is much gentleness in them. There is a hunger and thirst for righteousness in them. There is mercy in them. There is purity of heart in them. There are peacemakers among them. Precisely in these people who are at the end of their tether one can discover all these positive qualities. One simply has to develop an eye for them. One must look at them with the eyes of God – with the eyes of Jesus. Blessed are those who are incompetent in life. God wills to begin his kingdom on earth with them.

When I had got to this point my eyes fell on the gown. Anger came over me at the devaluation of morality and competence in life which I assumed to be behind this gown. And I hurled my quotation from Luther against it. For Luther himself saw in the Beatitudes an 'exposition of all the laws which have already been given and will ever be given', criteria for any ethics and morality. He saw in them pointers to a Christian life. What he said about the Beatitude on those who are pure in heart is particularly fine: it should open our eyes to the fact that we must 'look for God in the wretched, the errant and the toiling, on which God himself also looks: there we look on God, there the heart is pure and all pride is humbled'.

The Beatitudes teach us to see God in the poor: God's goodness in their goodness, God's mercy in their mercy, God's peace in their readiness for peace. The Beatitudes teach us to discover something that is already there – and that only becomes visible when we look on people with the eyes of Jesus, with the eyes of God, with the eyes of love.

So the Beatitude about the poor in spirit is addressed to all of us – to Protestants on both the left and right wings, to the fortunate and the unfortunate, to human beings who are broken and bowed down, and to the others who are Young, Attractive, Verbal, Intelligent and Social high level. So they are described in quite general terms in Matthew: 'Blessed are those who are poor in spirit' – not just 'Blessed are you who are poor in spirit.' For we should all become aware that there are positive possibilities in those in whom the will to life has been shattered.

The fortunate are to learn to perceive these possibilities in the unfortunate.

The unfortunate may discover them in themselves, even if here they have to fight against a penetrating voice which seeks to influence them, 'You're worthless. You're rubbish.' All of us, fortunate and unfortunate, are rubbish and clay, bits of matter organized in a complicated way. But it must be amazing rubbish that can be formed into the shapes that we have.

For all of us, fortunate and unfortunate, are the image of God. God has given us his life-giving spirit. This spirit puts us on our feet. It makes us walk upright. It brings us together so that we love one another. And where that happens, heaven begins on earth. There a great step is taken in our small life: the step into the kingdom of heaven. And you all may be involved in this: by doing good, by realizing the will of God all over the earth, even if you are poor in spirit, poor in courage to live, poor in the will to live. God has chosen all of you as citizens of his kingdom.

And if you hear God's word, if it reaches you, then you may be certain that you too are destined and chosen for this. So I beg you, listen to the words of Jesus. Let them enter your heart. Let them be louder than all the voices of envy and doubt. God himself is wooing you. God himself wants to find a way into you through these words. Listen once again to the good words of Jesus:

'Blessed are the Poor in Spirit'

Blessed are the poor in spirit,
for theirs is the kingdom of heaven.
Blessed are those who mourn,
for they will be comforted.
Blessed are the meek,
for they will inherit the earth.
Blessed are those who hunger and thirst for righteousness,
for they will be filled.

And may the peace of God which surpasses all our understanding keep your hearts and minds in Christ Jesus. Amen.

This sermon was given in St Peter's Church on 28 April 1991 as an introduction to a series of sermons on the Beatitudes.

Traces of Light

Being the light of the world is uncomfortable

(Matthew 5.13-16)

You are the salt of the earth; but if salt has lost its taste, how can its saltiness be restored? It is no longer good for anything, but is thrown out and trampled under foot. You are the light of the world. A city built on a hill cannot be hid. No one after lighting a lamp puts it under the bushel basket, but on the lampstand, and it gives light to all in the house. In the same way, let your light shine before others, so that they may see your good works and give glory to your Father in heaven.

Jesus tells you, 'You are the salt of the earth! You are the light of the world! Without you the earth is unpalatable. Without you the earth is dark. For without you people will forget to praise and thank God.'

That is a tremendous claim. It threatens to overwhelm us. So are these words true? Are Christians the salt of the earth, the light of the world?

And even if that were true – aren't these words the expression of an intolerably elitist consciousness?

Secularized contemporaries may find these words offensive. So they should be reminded that they have a parallel in the awareness of our time. Here, too, we find a tremendous self-awareness, except that no one attributes it to us. We attribute it to ourselves. We tell ourselves:

We are the light of the world. We human beings. Before us

there was darkness. Before us there was nature. Nature has produced us like a stepmother who does not care for her children. For she is indifferent to our joys and pains. We have emancipated ourselves from her by technology, and have mitigated her harshness by helping one another. So we have become sparks of meaning in a dark world – sparks of freedom, knowledge and love. We have made life worth living. We are the light of the world. And we are also the light of the world for others who have not reached our stage of enlightenment, and for dumb creatures.'

But there is also a counter-voice in us. This says:

We are the salt of the earth. Whether it remains palatable depends on us. Probably we have already over-salted the earth. Probably we have introduced something into it which goes against the system and is making everything collapse – equilibria which have arisen over millions of years. So we are anxious that the salt may be proving unusable and has to be thrown away – into the dustbin of evolution, which is where failed forms of life end up.

So we fluctuate between enlightened pride and anxiety about failure. And the two things are connected. If we bring sparks of meaning into the world, then everything depends on us – a phenomenon on the crust of a tiny planet, in a corner of the universe.

It is uncomfortable to be the salt of the earth and the light of the world. It is uncomfortable, no matter whether we translate the words of the Sermon on the Mount into a secularized consciousness without God or whether we hear them as the call of God. And yet there is a difference between the two forms of being uncomfortable. That's what I want to bring out. So I shall go through the threefold promise of light that we find at the beginning of the Gospel of Matthew (Matt.4.5 and 6).

The first promise of light in Matt.4 comes in the framework of the Sermon on the Mount. For the evangelist, an Old Testament promise is being fulfilled in the words and actions of Jesus – a promise of Isaiah. It runs:

The people who walked in darkness
have seen a great light;
those who lived in a land of deep darkness –
on them light has shined.

Before we are told 'You are the light of the world,' we hear the promise, 'The light has shined.' We need not create it. We need not bring it into the world. The light breaks into this world like dark clouds. At one point it breaks through for all: in Jesus, in his words and actions. In him a light shines which shines from the beginning, which lightens all human beings coming into the world. He is the light of God. God himself is light.

Here we have a decisive difference from the secularized consciousness without God: all light is the radiance of one great light, even if we do not want to perceive it, and even if we constantly forget and deny it. In everyday life we also forget that everything that we see is transformed sunlight – refracted by various surface structures, transformed into varied colours and figures. We think that things are a cause of what we see. Only by an intellectual effort which runs counter to our everyday consciousness do we understand that everything that penetrates to our skin by day ultimately has only one cause: the sun. Without it everything is night and darkness.

So too it is with God: we derive the colourful variety of the world from things and events in it, and forget the basis of all things; we forget that God's broken rays reach us through all things and events – every moment and everywhere. These rays are God's call, 'Where are you, Adam?', 'Where are you, Eve?' 'What are you doing with the infinite value of your life? What are you doing with the creation?' What are you doing with your brothers and sisters who are hungering and thirsting for righteousness? There is no place in the world where this call does not reach us. It is omnipresent, like light. It surrounds us like air. It moves us like a magnetic field. In it we live and move and have our being.

So we do not hurl the spark of meaning into a meaningless world, but it is kindled in us by the call of God. This call of God is the spark of meaning which kindles a bright light in the darkness – the light of truth, freedom and love. It makes us representatives of God's light in this world – also for others who do not praise and thank God. For dumb creatures as well.

The second promise of light at the beginning of the Sermon on the Mount in Matt.5 appoints us representatives of the light. Let me read it once again:

> *A city built on a hill cannot be hid. No one after lighting a lamp puts it under the bushel basket, but on the lampstand, and it gives light to all in the house. In the same way, let your light shine before others, so that they may see your good works and give glory to your Father in heaven.*

My first question here is, 'Doesn't this promise come too quickly? Those addressed were a people sitting in darkness and waiting longingly for the light. Now they themselves are to become light – those people who hear the Sermon on the Mount. They include the demon-possessed, the hobbling and the limping, the healthy and the sick, the strong and the weak, the disciples and the people. Or isn't that precisely the characteristic of God's light in this world? It shines particularly brightly when it falls on darkness, where it falls on a life in shadow. There in particular it can be seen all around. The recipients of light become the givers of light especially where darkness becomes light. But how is the light spread around?

The Sermon on the Mount says, 'by good works'. These are not to be put under a bushel, but made visible to all. Hence my second question. Doesn't that contradict later statements in the Sermon on the Mount? According to these, one is to give alms, pray and fast in secret. Here, by contrast, one is invited to do good works before all – not in secret but in public.

The contradiction is resolved if we become aware of what was understood in Judaism by 'good works' or 'works of love'. These were actions which required the commitment of one's own person, e.g. visiting the sick, offering hospitality to strangers, taking part in weddings and funerals, comforting those who mourn, making peace. Alms were sometimes distinguished from the other works of love because in giving them one could be unknown and remain in the background. Real works of love are only those that people do with their own person. Here one necessarily has to come into contact with those towards whom they are directed. Here by definition one cannot remain unknown. Here one must become visible, expose oneself and be in public view.

The third question follows directly from this. What public is envisaged? The Sermon on the Mount is often understood to relate only to the private sphere, indeed essentially to people's inner disposition. There the light of the gospel is to shine out. By contrast, three spheres are spoken of in our promise of light, directly and metaphorically:

First of all the world: Jesus' followers are not only to be light for their friends, but light for the world.

Secondly, we have the image of the 'city on the hill'. In antiquity a city (or polis) is identical with society and the state.

Finally, lampstands in the house are mentioned – in the smallest public sphere. But in antiquity the house is more than the family; it is the smallest business unit.

So it is said that the whole world, the whole of society, the whole house, is to be filled with the light of 'good works'. There are no limitations to the inner sphere, or to private life. What Christians do as a personal commitment is to shine out in all spheres. What they do to make peace, to ensure freedom, to further justice and to preserve the creation is all to become visible through their personal commitment.

But once again there is a question. Isn't that an intolerably elitist claim? To that I can only answer, 'No one can say.' We are the light of the world, we are the salt of the earth. Both these things are said to us. We are thought capable of it. People who formerly saw themselves sitting in darkness are capable of it. Those who are praised in the Beatitudes are thought capable of it: those poor in the power of life, the mourners, the meek, those who hunger and thirst after righteousness, those who are persecuted, all those who crouch in darkness are thought worthy of it. This is not an elite, but rather a counter-elite. However, it is true that God plans great things for such people. Through them he wills to make his light shine in the world! With them, and with us, he plans more than we think ourselves capable of.

And that is the great problem. Do we have the courage? Don't we often tell ourselves, 'I'm no great light. I'm only a very little light, certainly not the light of the world. I can't achieve anything. I'm small and helpless. I'm happy to survive and get through life, to get everything done properly. The "light of the world' is a bit too much for me.'

I could now comfort you by saying that we are not told that 'you' in the singular are the light of the world. The saying is in the plural. You together are the light of the world. You together are the salt of the earth. You are not alone. There are many whom God has called to spread his light, in every land and in every culture. There are Christians everywhere, though almost everywhere they are in the minority.

All that is true. Nevertheless, the saying is meant for you personally. That is shown by the third promise of light in Matthew 6. It is not formulated in the plural, but in the singular, and runs:

> *The eye is the lamp of the body. So, if your eye is healthy, your whole body will be full of light; but if your whole eye is unhealthy, your whole body will be full of darkness. If then the light in you is darkness, how great is the darkness.*

This third promise of light is tremendously important to me. It says, 'It also depends on you whether you see the light – and whether as a result your whole life (or as it says here, your whole body) becomes light.' It depends on you whether you become a light for others. For, first, you are completely responsible: just you and no one else. You are responsible for letting the light enter your body. You are responsible for perceiving when it shines. No one can compel you. No one can see for you. You are the only one who is capable of this. But if your eye is darkness, then everything becomes dark for you – even if the brightest light shines around you.

When it talks of the 'dark eye', the Sermon on the Mount is thinking of envy, i.e. of constant comparison with others – to the detriment of one's own life. This envy whispers to us:

'Everyone else is doing well. Only you are falling behind, in possessions and wealth' (that is what the Sermon on the Mount is thinking of).

Envy whispers to us, 'You're lacking in abilities and competence for bringing light into the world. Others do that, but you don't.'

'You're lacking in beauty and attractiveness. Others have it much easier in life.'

'You're lacking in love and care. All others are loved more than you are.'

The fatal thing is that such whispering is irrefutable. There are always people who are superior to us in possessions, capabilities and attractiveness. There are always people who had it easier in life than we did. The fatal thing is that we checkmate ourselves by comparing ourselves with them, so that as a result we darken our life and no longer see that a light shines in our lives and often also shines for others. And we don't notice it.

I also know from my own experiences how paralysing such irrational convictions can be. Hence my drastic advice: we have to drown such convictions afresh every day. They are part of the old Adam, who has been drowned in baptism. But I also know from experience that this old Adam is tough. He keeps coming back like a ghost to haunt you. If he does, practise driving away ghosts. You needn't be afraid of these ghosts. For you are a child of God, a child of light, and not a child of darkness.

And my second piece of advice is: of course you're small and tiny. But everything has a small beginning. Before the saying 'You are the light of the world' comes the saying 'You are the salt of the earth'. Before you become the light that fills the world, be prepared to be the salt: unnoticed, small, under-estimated, unattractive, but irreplaceable, vital to life and decisive for everything. For you are a grain of salt, a miraculous grain of salt.

However, despite all this it remains a fact that it is uncomfortable to be a grain of salt. It is uncomfortable to be called to be the light of the world. But it is a great opportunity, a threefold opportunity. The three promises of light tell us:

You are the light of the world. But you need not create this light. You do not introduce it to a grudging nature. It is there independently of you, in creation, in Jesus, in every human being who is transformed by God's love. This light is stronger than the shadow of death.

You are the light of the world. But not by belonging to an elite of the highly gifted. You are the light of the world: as normal people, as strong and weak. And as people who are anxious about dropping out of life and being useless. The light of God rests on such people.

You are the light of the world. But you do not need to kindle it. For the spark of meaning and love has been cast into your heart. You are bright if you let the light into you. You shine if your eye is not darkened.

Once again: you are the light of the world, for by your existence you make sure that people do not forget to praise and thank God.

This sermon was given in St Peter's Church, Heidelberg, on 21 July 1991.

Carefree Birds and Lilies and Our Anxieties About Them

(Matthew 6.25-34)

Therefore I tell you, do not worry about your life, what you will eat or what you will drink, or about your body, what you will wear. Is not life more than food, and the body more than clothing? Look at the birds of the air; they neither sow nor reap nor gather into barns, and yet your heavenly Father feeds them. Are you not of more value than they? And can any of you by worrying add a single hour to your span of life? And why do you worry about clothing? Consider the lilies of the field, how they grow; they neither toil nor spin, yet I tell you, even Solomon in all his glory was not clothed like one of these. But if God so clothes the grass of the field, which is alive today and tomorrow is thrown into the oven, will he not much more clothe you – you of little faith? Therefore do not worry, saying, 'What will we eat?' or 'What will we drink?' or 'What will we wear?' For it is the Gentiles who strive for all these things; and indeed your heavenly Father knows that you need all these things. But strive first for the kingdom of God and his righteousness, and all these things will be given to you as well. So do not worry about tomorrow, for tomorrow will bring worries of its own. Today's trouble is enough for today.

When I go down the main street and look at people's faces, I know that this stream of people coming towards me is a stream of anxieties and suffering. On the street I see too many expressionless faces which have been deadened by too much anxiety. On it I meet eyes that seem dead, burnt out by the cares of everyday life. Worn-out figures move along the street, ground down by the harshness of life. Prosperity in life presupposes that we have learned to cope with anxieties, so that we do not drown in the flood of cares, are not torn apart, are not crushed.

Our text contains four piece of advice on this. I shall begin with the least obvious thought in it, lead up to the most important, and from there return to the small and insignificant.

The first piece of advice relates to every single day: each day has its trouble. It is enough for us to be bothered about our present troubles – and not also future troubles, which we do not yet know but only guess at. We cannot barricade ourselves against anxieties. But we can limit our anxieties about future anxieties, as they poison life.

The second piece of advice relates to our whole life. Keep telling yourself that you cannot add a minute to your life or anyone else's by worrying. But you can darken many minutes in your life (and in the lives of your fellow human beings) by anxiety. Keep telling yourself, 'Death is inevitable.' It will come. It will come for you and those whom you love. But it is not inevitable that the thought of death should poison your life.

The third piece of advice directs our gaze beyond our life to the nature in which we are embedded. Birds and lilies know no anxieties. Shouldn't that be an example for us? An example of freedom from anxiety? However, precisely that has become a problem for us today: the birds of the air are emigrating because they cannot find any food here. We have to protect the lilies so that they do not die out. Even nature has become an object of our anxieties. We are anxious about it because we have destroyed its order. Bitter though this recognition is, it also contains a promise: if we respect the order of nature anew, then we can trust in it again. Then it will perhaps again become an example of how we can learn freedom from anxieties.

And finally there is the most important piece of advice. It points beyond the day, the individual life, beyond nature. It opens up the widest perspective. It opens up a view of the kingdom of God and God's righteousness, beyond the righteousness which is expected from the citizens of this kingdom and for which it makes them hunger and thirst. All life is an experiment in corresponding to God, from the slipper animalcule to *homo sapiens*. But only in human beings does the experiment become conscious. We are the only ones who can be seized beyond all other anxieties by this one anxiety, by hungering and thirsting after righteousness, after the doing of God's will in heaven and on earth. Because this anxiety can seize us, drive us and hurt us, we are worth more than the birds of the air. We are worth more than the lilies in the field. Before this great anxiety all other anxieties pale.

In recent months I have had many reasons for anxiety.

First, there was anxiety about my younger son, who wanted to work in a black township in South Africa but was confronted there, and is still confronted, with a wave of violence, murder and death threats. The blacks who became his friends lived daily with the anxiety that murder squads would appear and kill them. How we have to admire these people who do not let themselves be got down, who hunger and thirst for righteousness, for the most elementary of all righteousnesses, that of being recognized as human beings on an equal footing – finding clothing, food, education and work after having for decades been degraded to second- and third-class people in a racist dictatorship! Our petty anxieties fade in the face of this great anxiety.

Then recently there has been renewed anxiety about nature. The most recent reports on the ozone layer have demonstrated incontrovertibly that the ecological crisis is not a fashionable invention of postmodernity. It is reality. It will affect us all. That God makes his sun shine on the just and the unjust will perhaps soon no longer be a comfort but a danger. Yet the knowledge of this danger is also a comfort. Only this knowledge makes it possible for us to change our behaviour in time and avert the great catastrophe. Only this knowledge makes conversion possible, makes it possible for us to do justice to the creation as God requires this of us.

I was also consumed with anxiety about my old parents-in-law, who have become frail and decrepit. Old age can be bitter when it ends in confusion and depression of the kind that I can see in my father-in-law. And yet I know that it's no use complaining and consuming oneself in anxiety. Those of us who belong to a younger generation have the task of doing the little we can to support a life that is coming to an end. Once we accept that, and do not resist the fact that life, including our own, is coming to an end, this can be a fulfilling task.

And last but not least, each of us is anxious that we may not be able to perform our daily duties. In everyday life the little duties and deadlines keep towering up like great mountains. All those faced with examinations know the situation. The stuff piles up. One can only get though it by dividing it into small portions. A bit of preparation each day is enough. However, it's an illusion to think that after the examination everything will change. No, life is one great examination. The demands keep piling up. And that is true of every day. It is enough to cope with its anxieties. And if things cannot be otherwise, then I live by the slogan that my first obligation is not to do what is not absolutely necessary. As a result, I usually have a bit more room. Room, also, to dream. Room to reflect on birds and lilies and on what Jesus says about birds and lilies.

Over these last months I've often gone down the main street. But I've found that this flood of people is not just a stream of anxiety and sorrow. Sometimes these people even make me feel good. Indeed, I can be electrified by the thought that the same will to live is pulsating in all of them, just as it is in me. It is often hidden, covered over and damaged. But it keeps filling empty faces with new spirit. It keeps making dulled eyes light up again. It gives worn-out people new energy. And then I feel that I am allied with a great power against all anxieties. I feel it in me and around me. It pulsates in my life and in the life that surrounds me. But it is more than all this life. It is alive in everything: in the smallest particles and in the whole cosmos, in the birds and sparrows, the grains of corn and the lilies.

When I feel this power, I am happy. So my wish is that you should all be able to feel this power – an antidote to all cares. This power is the peace of God which passes all our understanding. May it keep your hearts and minds in Christ

103

Jesus. Amen.

This sermon was given at the Wednesday morning service at St Peter's Church, Heidelberg, on 12 February 1992 – shortly before the end of the semester, when teachers and students are usually under pressure from deadlines and some examinations are due. One of my sons was in South Africa at this time, where he was experiencing the increasing wave of violence. It also threatened his closest contacts, above all Prince M.Mhlambi, the young South African civil rights leader and head of the Johannesburg slum settlement of Phola Park. At the beginning of 1992 they had a short holiday together on the south coast. On 10 October 1992, after my son had returned to Germany, Prince M.Mhlambi and three other young men were shot by a murder squad while they were on a car journey.

The Power of Consensus

or, Can Church Discipline be Humane?

(Matthew 18.15-20)

If your brother sins against you, go and point out the fault when the two of you are alone. If he listens to you, you have regained him. But if you are not listened to, take one or two others along with you, so that every word may be confirmed by the evidence of two or three witnesses. If he refuses to listen to them, tell it to the community; and if he refuses to listen even to the community, let such a one be to you as Gentile and a tax collector. Truly I tell you, whatever you bind on earth will be bound in heaven, and whatever you loose on earth will be loosed in heaven. Again, truly I tell you, if two of you agree on earth about anything you ask, it will be done for you by my Father in heaven. For where two or three are gathered in my name, I am there among them.

There are certainly people among us who have at some time been excluded from a group, whether through formal proceedings or through general social pressure. That has happened me twice: once in a Christian youth group, and the second time in my first job. When I read the rule about exclusion in the Gospel of Matthew just now, that went through my head. Exclusions are often bound up with painful experiences and leave wounds. Against the background of my own experiences, Matthew's rules for exclusion seem to me to be quite human. These rules can be summed up under two headings: 1. 'All exclusions can be reviewed; 2. 'The power of consensus in the community'.

The first concern of the rules is that all exclusions can be reviewed. The context makes that clear. Before this comes the parable of the lost sheep – the opposite of the procedure for exclusions. It is about the attempt to re-integrate someone who has distanced himself. There follows the invitation to unlimited forgiveness. We are to forgive our brothers not only seven but seventy-seven times. Whenever the person who is excluded repents, he is welcome, and is to be forgiven.

So the Gospel of Matthew formulates both before this passage and after it a concern to maintain communion with every member of the community – and to do everything, really everything, to make that possible. The fact that in the middle there is nevertheless mention of necessary exclusion shows all the more clearly that there are limits to community. Even a group which wants to resolve its conflicts through forgiveness and feels especially indebted to its lost sheep knows that it cannot avoid specifying when and under what conditions it must exclude someone.

But if that is already unavoidable, the exclusion must take place fairly, in three stages.

First there is the confidential conversation. That's a good rule. Instead of gossiping all round the community about the problematical case, the person concerned must be spoken with privately. That's an opportunity for the 'accused'; it can remove misunderstandings. But it's also an opportunity for the accusers, who can withdraw a charge if it proves false. The public reputation of both parties remains undamaged.

Secondly, the Matthaean rules for exclusions provide for a conversation in the presence of two witnesses. That, too, is a good thing. I can remember that in one of my conflicts I was simply fighting to present the misdemeanour I was said to have committed to two witnesses. No such conversation took place. I never learned what was held against me.

And finally the third stage. This consists in a discussion before the whole community. That's an excellent rule. It prevents a small group from imposing its interests on the community by excluding individuals. If we exclude anyone, the exclusion must be imposed by all and be defended before all. When I was being sacked from a Christian youth group I had the opportunity to speak to the whole group. I was rehabilitated – and this was rather painful for my opponents. In my second sacking I didn't have this opportunity.

It is clear that only in anticipation of a consensus, only in the conviction that all members of the group assent to the exclusion (even if they are not perhaps actually involved in it), can an exclusion be implemented. This consensus has great force. And that is the second theme of the text: 'the power of consensus in the community'. This power is so great that it is almost uncanny. We are told that 'what you bind on earth will also be bound in heaven'. All decisions about acceptance and rejection, all decisions about doctrinal questions, are valid if they are made by a consensus. Heaven, i.e. God himself, also accepts them. Doesn't that overvalue a consensus among human beings? Can't even the whole community err in the most harmonious consensus? And hasn't it often erred?

Who would dispute that? Yet we are left with nothing better on earth than the search for a consensus. We remain tied to it, even if one of us thinks that we have direct access to absolute truth – and perhaps even does have it.

I often explain that to myself with a story about Rabbi Eliezer ben Hyrcanus. He differed from the consensus of the other rabbinical scholars on a relatively insignificant matter of purity – and could not convince his colleagues, though he could offer a series of miracles to support his thesis.

Rabbi Eliezer said, 'If the law is as I believe, then let this tree tell us.' And behold, the tree transplanted itself 100 ells of its own accord. But the other scholars only said, 'That proves nothing.'

Then he said, 'If I am right, let the stream say it,' and in fact the stream suddenly flowed uphill. But the others only said, 'That proves nothing.'

Then Eliezer said, 'If the law is as I believe, then let these walls say it.' Thereupon the walls fell in. But one of the rabbis objected to the walls, 'How can you fall in when scholars are arguing?' And out of respect for them, the walls raised themselves up again – but only half way. For out of respect for Rabbi Eliezer they did not want to raise themselves completely.

Finally Eliezer said, 'A voice from heaven shall decide,' and a voice rang out from heaven, saying, 'What do you have against Rabbi Eliezer? The law is as he says.'

But the rabbis were not at all impressed. They said, 'In the law it is written, "You shall decide by majority opinion."' And they maintained their view.

A short time afterwards, one of them met the prophet Elijah, who had been informed in heaven about all the proceedings, and asked him, 'What did God himself say when we had our dispute?' Elijah replied, 'God smiled and said, "My children have got the better of me, my children have got the better of me."'

This story tells us that God respects the consensus of his children, even when it is objectively false. God waits patiently until the arguments among human beings arrive at the truth. This non-authoritarian procedure is more important to God than any absolute truth, no matter how many miracles support it.

The consensus that is found in this way in fact has great force. The Gospel of Matthew says of it, 'If two of you agree on earth about anything you ask, it will be done for you by my Father in heaven.'

This saying first of all makes a quite unrealistic promise. Even the agreement of two Christians in prayer will lead to that prayer being heard. Here agreement with the neighbour is a truly miraculous force.

But before we therefore brush the saying aside as a bizarre exaggeration, we should read on, for the assurance that prayer will be heard is followed by the reason why: 'For where two or three are gathered in my name, I am there among them.' Anyone who is in agreement with a fellow Christian and presents the same concern from the depths of his or her heart is given at least one promise: Jesus is with him or her. Jesus is where two or three Christians agree. His spirit is a spirit of accord, which penetrates the depths of the heart. And whether or not our wishes and petitions are fulfilled, one wish is always fulfilled: Jesus' spirit has taken hold of us where we agree.

Precisely for that reason we must do everything we can to seek and maintain such agreement. Precisely for that reason we must go after the lost sheep, those who no longer agree with us. Precisely for that reason we must forgive the other without limit – if it furthers the chance of such agreement. Precisely for that reason consensus is a piece of heaven on earth.

Where we trace this accord of wishes and concerns, we trace something of the peace of God. And may this peace of God which surpasses all our understanding keep your heart and mind in Christ Jesus. Amen.

This sermon was given on 4 July 1990 at the Wednesday morning service in St Peter's Church, Heidelberg. My exclusion from a Christian youth group was a matter of the usual tensions between various tendencies: on the one hand a youth culture more orientated on the youth movement (with an anti-authoritarian accent), and on the other youth work more orientated on the Boy Scout Movement, which had a strong orientation on discipline and achievement. I represented the first tendency; among other things I was against hoisting the German national flag on journeys abroad. My dismissal from my first job still seems to be absurd. I was ready and willing to go after a year. The dispute turned primarily on the fact that I wanted to have a reason for the premature ending of my post. The rabbinic tradition about Rabbi Eliezer ben Hyrcanus appears in the Babylonian Talmud, in Tractate Baba Mezia 59b.

'What you have done for the least of my brothers...'

Justice in an unjust world

(Matthew 25.31-46)

When the Son of Man comes in his glory, and all the angels with him, then he will sit on the throne of his glory. All the nations will be gathered before him, and he will separate people one from another as a shepherd separates the sheep from the goats, and he will put the sheep at his right hand and the goats at the left. Then the king will say to those at his right hand, 'Come, you that are blessed by my Father, inherit the kingdom prepared for you from the foundation of the world; for I was hungry and you gave me food, I was thirsty and you gave me something to drink, I was a stranger and you welcomed me, I was naked and you gave me clothing, I was sick and you took care of me, I was in prison and you visited me.' Then the righteous will answer him, 'Lord, when was it that we saw you hungry and gave you food, or thirsty and gave you something to drink? And when was it that we saw you a stranger and welcomed you, or naked and gave you clothing? And when was it that we saw you sick or in prison and visited you?' And the king will answer them, 'Truly I tell you, just as you did it to one of the least of these my brothers, you did it to me.' And he will say to those at his left hand, 'You that are accursed, depart from me into the eternal fire prepared for the devil and his angels; for I was hungry and you gave me no food, I was thirsty and you gave me nothing to drink, I was a stranger and you did not welcome me, naked and you did not give me clothing, sick and in prison and you did not visit me.' Then they also will answer, 'Lord, when was it that we saw you hungry or thirsty or sick or in prison and did not take care of you?' Then he will answer them, 'Truly I tell you, just as you did not to it to one of the least of these, you did not do it to me.' And these will go away into eternal punishment, but the righteous into eternal life.

The Gospel of Matthew ends the discourses of Jesus with a discourse about the last judgment. At the end, before the supreme judge, human beings who have helped the least of their fellows will be judged righteous. For in these fellow human beings the last judge has encountered them. This discourse contains a great vision of justice. Matthew knows that this vision has metaphorical features. He compares the activity of the judge to that of a shepherd who separates the sheep and the goats, in order to slaughter the goats which give no milk and to continue to rear the sheep. That is how vividly he depicts the judgment of the world. For the evangelist, despite all the poetic features, this is more than a picture. He believes in a judgment in a literal sense. But I am certain that not all of us are prepared to follow the evangelist here. There are those who will have difficulties in believing in a judge of the world who divides human beings like sheep and goats, some to enter eternal life and others to be condemned to eternal punishment. There are those who will rightly ask, 'Isn't that a religious poem, a myth? A myth which represents a new idea of justice in the form of a fantasy of the end time?' Perhaps. Be that as it may, I love this myth.

To explain my love of this myth, let me tell a modern myth about justice. Its features are as poetic as the picture of the judge of the world in the Gospel of Matthew. Whereas with Matthew we find ourselves at the end of the ages, this myth takes us into a state before our birth – before all times, before the beginning of history.

This myth of primal time says: The world has still to be created. We are all gathered together in this before-time and have the task of sketching out a just world, i.e. a world in which the fortunes of life and the good things of the earth are justly distributed. After long discussion we agree on the following procedure: a just world will have to present such an appearance

111

that the distribution of destinies and the good things of life can be accepted in it by anyone – on one presupposition: all must be able to accept it without knowing what role and what destiny they will be given. Everyone must reckon with the possibility of being given the role of 'the least of all human beings'. Moreover, all must be able to affirm their roles and the distribution of all destinies even if they find themselves right at the bottom. What is decisive for this sketch of a just world is not knowing the future distribution of destinies. A 'veil of ignorance' is decisive.

Incidentally, we all know this principle of justice. If we have to share a cake we have it cut by someone who must be the last to choose a piece. That person must then take into account that if everyone else chooses the biggest piece available, the smallest piece will be left.There's a real motive for dividing the cake equally and fairly!

Life isn't a cake which can be divided fairly in this way (in approximately equal pieces). Happiness and unhappiness, health and sickness, power, possessions and education, are unfairly divided. The poetic story of the sketching out of a just world in primal times is meant to help us to discover how we can do justice even on the presupposition that the opportunities of life have been distributed fairly. The criterion for this justice is the fate of the least, those who have come off worst, and the decisive question to us is: Would we affirm the destiny of these least as our own destiny?

The myth of primal time which I have just told was constructed by a modern philosopher, John Rawls, to present his principle of justice. Of course he doesn't believe literally that before all time people could have discussed and decided the shape of the world. Nevertheless, he can express his truth better with his poetic image (which is totally fictional) than with abstract ideas. The Gospel of Matthew does not tell any story of primal times. It presents a vision of the end-time. Anyone who has difficulties with its image of the last judgment can first of all take it as poetic image which contains a truth about justice. However, this image allows us to discover more than a universal principle of justice. We discover a justice which is to stand before an ultimate authority, God himself. We discover what it means to speak of God as judge.

Before we decipher the picture of the judge of the world, in the first part of this Bible study I want you yourselves to adopt the role of judge, namely in judging the correct interpretation of this text. Two parties are arguing over it. The dispute is unresolved. We must attempt to listen to these parties like a neutral judge and make the best judgment we can.

In the second part we shall abandon this role of judge and adopt the role of those who are summoned to judgment. We want to understand what the great role of judge involves – with the image of the judge of the world. That is one of the great images that we apply to God – alongside images of father and mother, king and friend, marriage and covenant partner.

In the third part we shall seek once again to exchange roles: we shall seek to become observers of the process. Our aim is to discover what is being conveyed by the image of the last judgment of the world – as compared with the modern primal-time myth of justice. Both poetic images are related. In both, the veil of ignorance plays a central role. The human beings before the creation of the world do not know what role they are to adopt in the world that they have constructed. The human beings facing the judge of the world do not know the role in which this judge has encountered them. If two such different images of justice correspond, then mustn't a truth be hidden in them? But what truth? And where is the difference despite this agreement?

I

First of all, let's imagine ourselves as an exegetical tribunal which has to decide on true and false interpretations. Two biblical scholars are facing this tribunal. The first is defending an interpretation of this text in terms of the whole of humankind, the second an interpretation in terms of the church. The first regards a universalist exegesis as correct, the second defends a particularistic exegesis. Let's listen to both of them, the universalist and the particularist.

The universalist outlines his position like this. All human beings, whether they are Jews, Gentiles or Christians, will be judged by God in accordance with the same criterion: have you or have you not helped people in need? In his discourse the evangelist Matthew is answering the age-old question: What happens before God to those who do not believe in him? What happens to the 'pagans'? Are they lost simply because the preaching has not reached them? Or because they have not come to believe? His answer is: They are by no means lost. Even if Christ has not encountered them; even if they have heard nothing of him, have not believed in him, he has encountered them unbeknown in all who are in need of help. The judge of the world appears incognito in the face of every human being. All those who help people in need are just.

The particularist presents his counter-thesis. The story of the judgment of the world does not speak of a judgment on all human beings but only of a judgment on the Gentiles. They are not measured by what they have done to those in need but by what they have done to the brothers of Jesus. These brothers are the same disciples who are sent out with the promise, 'Whoever welcomes you welcomes me, and whoever welcomes me welcomes the one who sent me' (Matt.10.40). The image of the judgment of the world is meant to comfort the community of Jesus: its members will indeed have to suffer much in the world from others – hunger, thirst, rejection, prison – but they are to know that God will punish those who refuse them help. God will reward those who help them. Nor is the image about good people doing good for its own sake, without recognizing the judge of the world, without seeing the consequences. On the contrary, talk of the judgment of the world is meant to make these consequences plain. It seeks to hold out a prospect of reward for the just.

The universalist protests that the vision of the judgment of the world is narrowed in a sectarian way by this interpretation, as if it were about the community edifying itself with the thought of how important it is. In the judgment of the world, all other people are measured by how they behave towards us. This interpretation of the 'least of the brothers' in terms of Christians and missionaries comes to grief on one simple consideration: what remarkable missionaries they would be who allowed themselves to be helped without saying that this help was help for God's cause! What remarkable Christians they would be who left their rescuers ignorant of having helped the brothers and sisters of Jesus! When the disciples are sent out on a mission, they are not only told, 'Whoever welcomes you welcomes me', but also, 'Whoever welcomes a prophet *because* he is a prophet, whoever welcomes a righteous person *because* he is a righteous person, and whoever gives even a cup of cold water to one of these little ones *because* he is a disciple, will receive his reward' (Matt.10.40-42). It is always presupposed that those who are giving help know that they are helping Christians active in the name of Jesus. By contrast, the human beings in the judgment of the world do not know with whom they are dealing. They help the 'least', not because they are prophets, righteous and disciples, but because they are in need. These least are therefore *all* who suffer. And *all* human beings are measured by their attitude towards them. Where Matthew emphatically speaks not only of 'nations', but of *all* nations, he is leaving no one out. At any rate, the 'sheep' whom the Son of Man tends belong to these nations. However, sheep and flock are a stereotyped image of Israel or the church.

The particularist does not give up, but retorts energetically that the universalist interpretation in terms of all human beings and all those in need is wishful thinking. Exegesis is committed to the truth, even if doesn't suit us. It is exegetical truth that in an early Christian text, 'brothers of the Son of Man' can only mean Christians. If the Son of Man, Jesus himself, is secretly present in these brothers of the Son of Man, then belief in the risen Christ is presupposed: for only the risen Christ can be mysteriously present in his community. So here the church is being spoken of.

The universalist counters that the particularist exegesis is also wishful thinking (or better, an expression of anxiety). There are theologians who are afraid of too much humanism in the Bible. They are afraid that the church and faith will become superfluous if in the end all that matters is whether human beings have helped other human beings. and have done so even without religious motivation, without wanting to help the Son of Man (i.e. Jesus), wanting only to help others.

What shall we say about this dispute between the biblical interpreters? Since I must be represent the jury for everyone, let me propose a settlement: both parties are right, but not in the way that they assume. The texts of the Bible have often undergone development. The particularistic interpretation has a true insight into the early stage of the development of the text (or the relevant material here). But the text as we now have it in Matthew shows signs of a revision in the direction of a universalistic view. So let me offer two interpretations.

My first interpretation, which relates to the original text, has only one presupposition: this text was originally spoken by a Jew to Jews. My question is, what did a Jewish audience understand by 'all nations' and 'brothers'? In my view the answer isn't difficult.

Certainly many interpreters believe that the term 'brother' only fits Christians. There is no evidence in Judaism that the Israelites were imagined to be brothers of God or of the Son of Man. Reflecting on this, it struck me that the name 'brother' appears in the text precisely where the judge of the world is called 'king'. In v.40 it is said, 'And the *king* will answer them, "Truly I tell you, just as you did it to one of the least of these my *brothers*, you did it to me."' My question is, where is it conceivable that a king should call his subjects 'brothers'? That in itself is striking. The end of kingly rule in Europe was once proclaimed with the slogan 'Freedom, equality, *brotherhood*'. Monarchy and brotherhood do not go together. However, anyone who knows the Bible knows that in the law of the king in Deuteronomy 17 the king is admonished not to exalt himself above his brothers. He is to come from the 'brothers', i.e. the people whom he is to rule. In Israel, the king could be called

116

one brother among others. Israel corrected the power of the king with the appeal to brotherhood. Talk of the judgment of the world now speaks not of a past king of Israel but of the future messianic king. His brothers are the Israelites. But that means that the 'nations' who are contrasted with these brothers are Gentiles, i.e. non-Israelites.

In that case, what was the original point of the text? To understand that, we need to know that in Israel some circles expected a future king who would rescue Israel from the Gentiles. Many imagined this as a great judgment on the Gentiles. They had oppressed Israel for a long time, so now they were to be punished for it. But others gave the Gentiles a chance. In Psalms of Solomon 17, the most important text about the Jewish messianic expectation, first of all we find sharp statements about the Gentiles, but in the end the Gentiles will stream to Zion and bring the exhausted Israelites with them from the Diaspora. They will help the dispersed Jews. Our text goes yet further in this direction: the messiah of Israel will measure all Gentiles by what they have done for the oppressed Jews, whether they have helped them when they were hungry, thirsty, naked, strangers, sick and in prison. Here all are judged by criteria which are well known to them. For there is much evidence that the good deeds enumerated belong to the ethos of all nations. The formulations from Egypt are particularly impressive.

I could imagine that with this talk of the judgment of the world Jesus was criticizing a narrow nationalistic attitude which exists in any people – and also existed among Jews. He taught that the other nations also have a chance in the last judgment. And in saying this he followed a more liberal tendency in Judaism.

However, for us the text takes on a new meaning. We are Gentiles. According to this text we shall all be judged by our attitude to Jews. Over a long history, our attitude to Judaism has in fact become a criterion for humanity. Whether we overcome the poison of antisemitism, whether we resist this evil which keeps recurring, has become a decisive factor. Do we support Jews where they are in need?

So the particularistic interpretation is right in principle (for the original version of the text). But it is wrong, because it was not originally the church, but Israel, that the text had in mind.

Now to the second interpretation. The evangelist Matthew himself understood talk of the judgment of the world afresh, in universalistic terms. By 'brothers' of the Son of Man he is thinking of all human beings. He twice speaks of these brothers and those in need of help. The first time (in v.40) he describes them as 'the least of my brothers', the second time only as 'these least' (v.45). So he omits the term 'brother' in the repetition. He is therefore less concerned with any 'affinity' and group membership than with the fact that these people are the least. It has been objected that in the second part of the text with its many repetitions, Matthew in any case abbreviates. The transition from the 'least of my brothers' to 'the least' is said to be an expression of this general tendency to abbreviate, a stylistic variation the content of which cannot therefore be evaluated. That does not work. On the contrary, precisely when we take this tendency to abbreviate into account, we note that the expression 'the least of my brothers' can be abbreviated in two ways, either to 'What you have done to my brother you have done to me' (which makes good sense, since brothers are part of oneself) or, 'What you have done to these least you have done to me' – a very bold statement in the mouth of the judge of the world, who has a quite superior position, who does not belong among the least, and cannot be surpassed by anyone in power and status. By choosing the second possibility, in my view Matthew makes it clear that for him the decisive thing is that this passage is about insignificant people in need of help. So he is not saying that the brothers of Jesus are insignificant and in need, but that the insignificant and those in need are the brothers of Jesus.

Thus just as we may doubt whether with 'the least' Matthew is thinking exclusively of Christians, so we may doubt whether with 'all nations' he is thinking exclusively of non-Christians. For at the time of the evangelist Matthew, part of all the nations had become Christians. At the end of his Gospel the disciples are given the task of making disciples of all nations. By the last judgment many from the nations will have become Christians. When 'all nations' are gathered together in the last judgment, Christians too will doubtless be among them. They, too, are judged – by the same criterion as that by which all human beings are judged.

So our judgment is that both exegetical parties are right. Matthew is revising in a universalist direction a discourse about the last judgment which was originally concentrated solely on Israel: he is thinking of all human beings and all those in need.

II

So far we have played judges in the dispute between the biblical scholars. But now we must give up the role of judge to recognize ourselves as human beings who themselves stand before a tribunal. This change of role does not come easily. But it is already being prepared for where we take our role as judges quite seriously. Perhaps you may have noticed that the exegetical judge in the end attempts to let the texts speak for themselves. He addresses the disputed questions to the texts in such a way as to coax a verdict out of them, a kind of judgment which he only pronounces, but does not make by his own standards.

I want to generalize this observation in order to demonstrate what experiences have entered into the images of the supreme judgment.

The first generalizing step relates to the academic disciplines as a whole. They, too, are often said to be judgments about the truth. Here, too, first of all people think that the scholar is the judge who listens impartially to all the witnesses, and then makes a judgment. In reality things are different. Not only exegesis, but all science attempts to formulate questions and hypotheses in such a way that the subject-matter itself provides an answer. In the last resort, reality is to decide whether a conjecture is tenable or not. The whole of science is a methodical attempt to make reality the judge of our notions and surmises.

A second generalizing step leads from science to the whole of life. The whole of life is trial and error. We shape it experimentally in one way or another – and hope that reality will give us the certainty that things are like this and not otherwise. We know all too well that reality is prone to mistakes and gives much room to what is nonsensical, useless and wrong. But if in the long run we ignore the basic conditions of reality in principle, they will rebound on us in catastrophes. So we are always zealously concerned to decode the repercussions of our actions from reality – with a view to a concealed judgment: that's all right and that isn't.

A third step finally takes us to religion: religion and faith make us aware of this basic feature of all life. We are through and through a product of an overall reality which is superior to us. This reality has produced us and sustains us, and we are subject to its order – in thoughts, words and actions. Religion makes us sensitive to this all-embracing dependence. It makes us aware that the whole of life is a kind of trial in which our ideas, words and works are tested. But above all it transforms a fate which is endured passively into a process which is carried out deliberately, by addressing as God the ground of the overall reality which brings us forth. At every moment we stand before God's judgment seat. When our life is finished, all that remains of this life is what is subject to the judgment of God. God is our judge.

Here the religions which imagine God as judge – and they also include the biblical religion – begin from too simple a picture. They believe that God as judge rewards the successful forms of life and rejects unsuccessful forms of life. But this picture of 'God the judge' changes in the course of a long history with God. It changes under the pressure of the decisive question that we put to any judge. Is the judge just? Is God just? Don't things go amazingly well with the rogues and often badly with the good? Is suffering on earth compatible with the notion of a just God?

The New Testament has no theoretical answer to this. But time and again it offers suggestions which can help us to deal with this question in practice, to endure the impossibility of resolving it, and to transform the torment contained in it into something good. Here I shall mention only the promptings that I find in the Gospel of Matthew, which come to a climax in this text about the judgment of the world.

You ask, 'If God is a just judge, why do the rogues fare so well?' What I read about this in the Gospel of Matthew is that God makes his sun rise on both the good and the bad, and makes the rain fall on both the just and the unjust. Regard it as a sign of God's generosity and goodness that he allows rogues to live well. Above all, learn a lesson from it. Love even your enemies in the same sovereign way in which God loves them, even the repulsive people, the rogues great and small.

You ask, 'If God is a just judge, why are the good so unfairly rewarded for their efforts? One person is successful and another suffers!' Read the parable of the labourers in the vineyard in the Gospel of Matthew. Some have toiled all day, others less, and the last only for a brief hour before work comes to an end – but all get the same wages. Are you envious because God is gracious to these last workers, who have had to put in very little effort? You ask, 'If God is a just judge, why is God so inconsistent that he keeps giving rogues another chance? Not only once, but seven times, indeed seventy-seven times?' Just think, you too profit from this divine inconsistency. For sometimes you too are a little rogue. Read the parable of the unmerciful servant who is let off paying a large sum of money, but demands a small sum from his fellow servant! Do you want to behave like that? With divine inconsistency God has also forgiven your wickednesses, great and small – and now are you going to insist that a fellow human being must be punished severely by God for his wickednesses, great or small?

And finally, you ask, 'But what am I to say to those who have failed to get their due in this world? Am I to tell them that it is God's will that they are faring worse than others? That they shouldn't be envious of the others who have more? Wouldn't that be cynical?' You're right. That wouldn't just be cynical. It is cynical. Read the discourse about the great judgment on the world: where you meet people who have come off worst, strangers, the sick and those in prison, people who don't have enough to eat, to drink or to wear, then know that in them you are meeting God. If you turn away from them cynically, then you are turning away from God himself. Their need is God's call.

Here the judge himself is taking the role of those on whom he is passing judgment. He himself is taking the role of those who are hungry and thirsty, sick and naked, and sitting in prison. He does not attempt to present the world as just. Rather he discloses the injustice of the world – without beautifying it, toning it down, trivializing it. He shows that this world is cruel. It is so cruel that in it God himself goes to the dogs. God goes to the dogs in all those who hunger and thirst, who are naked and sick, who are stuck in prison. But precisely for that reason God expects great things of you: God wants you not to be overcome or paralysed by the injustice of the world. God wants this injustice to be a powerful provocation which leads you to show humanity, which leads you to goodness, to overcome injustice and envy. If you do that, you belong among the just and the blessed from whom a warm light shines on a cold world.

To put it in rather more abstract terms, the images and narratives of the Bible constantly call to mind the ethical irrationality of the world. But these images and narratives seek to interpret this irrational world in such a way that it becomes the motive for ethical action and makes self-respect possible even in the greatest suffering. If that happens, the questions shift for us. Our first question then is no longer, 'Is the world just?', 'Is God just, if the opportunities in life are distributed so differently?' It is, 'Are we among the just?' 'Are we among those who have not missed God's call in the distress of others – the strangers, the sick and those in prison?' No one requires us to transform the whole world into a just world. Sometimes we have already done a great deal if we have not abandoned those who suffer, if we are simply with them.

You may perhaps ask, 'But what if things are going badly with me, if life is intolerable, if everything is going wrong, if everything is miserable?' Then read the Gospel of Matthew to

122

the end. Read the passion of Jesus. And the Gethsemane story. God himself shares in Jesus' anguish, death and pain. God suffers with his creatures in everything. God also suffers with you.

The decisive thing is that we should follow God in such a change of roles, from God right up there to God right down here. Then we shall also find it easier to affirm our own change of role: from judges of the world to people facing judgment. Of course we would much prefer to maintain some kind of role as judges. We want to examine the world, interrogate witnesses and ultimately declare it just or unjust. But in fact we are always already those under examination, the witnesses, those who are listening to the verdict on them. All our life is trial and error, in an attempt to be in harmony with God. The traditional image of God as judge from which we began says that God selects the successful attempts of our life and rejects the unsuccessful attempts. The new image of God as judge which we get from Matthew 26 says that God changes the criteria in a surprising way. God himself takes sides with apparently unsuccessful life. And God measures successful life by whether it has been lived in solidarity with the weak, hungry, sick and those in prison. God is a judge who himself takes the side of those whom some see as under judgment. God is judge in quite a different way from what we believed.

That is the justice which is outlined in this myth of a final judgment. It is a remarkable justice. Let's compare it yet again with another conception of justice.

III

Let's exchange roles once again. Finally let's understand ourselves once again as observers and analysts of those processes which are concerned with justice. Let's once again compare the justice of Matthew 25 with the justice in the modern primal-time myth which I related at the beginning. I believe that the two images and myths are complementary.

They have two things in common. First the 'veil of ignorance' that I have already mentioned. The people before all time do not know what role they will one day occupy in life. The people at the end of time in the great judgment of the world do not know in what role the judge of the world encountered them. Then there is a second common feature: in both cases the criterion for justice is the 'least', those who have got off worst in the distribution of opportunities in life. Their fate is the test of whether justice rules or not. Our attitude to them will show whether we are just or not. Justice does not show itself in the prosperity of the largest possible number of people, but rather in the minority of those who are right at the bottom of the pile. Nevertheless, two differences remain.

The people in primal time imagine what role they themselves will one day have – and after that they prepare their sketch of a just world. By contrast, the people before the world judgment are confronted with the fact that the judge of the world himself appears in the role of the other. It is not their own fate, possible or real, that becomes the criterion for justice, but the fate of the other. The two perspectives are not irreconcilable. But how might these two stories go if we were to combine both perspectives?

First of all the story of primal time. When the people were gathered together before history to sketch out a just world they agreed on the following principle for constructing a just world. They were sketching out a world in which everyone had to reckon with the possibility that the one who was encountered as the most insignificant person would one day occupy the highest place – with power over life and death. So the question was no longer, 'What can we expect of the least, so that we could even accept their role ourselves?', but, 'What can we expect of the person in the highest position if that person encounters us in the role of the least?"

And how could the story of the end-time be retold? Imagine that at the end of time the judge of the world gathers everyone together and offers them the possibility of returning to life. He shows them the world and offers them the lowliest role in the world. They reply, 'O no, we don't want that. A dog's life like that is quite intolerable for us. We'd rather not live at all.' Then the judge will ask them, 'And what did you do in your life to make such a dog's life more tolerable for other people?' 'What did you do to make such a dog's life a human life, which you too could accept?'

Both perspectives on justice can be combined. But it is typical that the philosophical myth asks what we can expect of ourselves, while the biblical myth asks what can we expect of others – the other person who is so infinitely valuable that God himself appears in him or her. Both are compatible. For the Bible also says, 'Love your neighbour as yourself. Make what you expect for yourself the criterion for what you expect for others. Make what you want for yourself the guideline for what you do to others.'

But a second difference remains. The philosophical myth is a story of primal time, the biblical narrative a story of the end-time. According to the primal-time myth, human beings have an opportunity to collaborate in the construction of the world. The conditions under which we live are imagined as being such that we could have helped to construct them. We appear as creators. The world becomes tolerable for us on the presupposition that we were able to have a say in its construction. That sounds very modern: we are the technicians of the world and justice.

The end-time myth is different: here we do not appear in the active role of shapers, but in the passive role of those on whom judgment is passed. We have had no say in the construction of the world. We found it there. And in it we found the hungry, thirsty and naked, the strangers, prisoners and the sick. We did not want it that way. No one asked us first. Bur our justice is shown by the way in which we deal with this world which was there before us and the people in it. What do we make of it, although we could have no say in setting the whole thing up?

This myth of the end-time has the advantage of being more realistic. For in fact life's like that. We didn't choose it. We ourselves didn't lay down its basic conditions. We can only say yes to it afterwards. But here too the difference is not insurmountable. Beyond question, the world was made without us. But it was made by God in such a way that in the course of a long evolution the human being emerged – the first creature that might understand itself to be a co-creator. God gave us a programme which is, 'Act as though you shared the responsibility for the further course of the world.' The human being is the one who is created co-creator with God. God has entrusted human beings with helping to create his justice.

If I may make one final comment as a small, insignificant co-creator of this justice, I would say that the distinction between just and unjust cannot be made in personal terms, as a division between sheep and goats. There is a little goat in each of us – including the saints. And there is a little sheep in each of us, including the greatest rogues, if only in the small child that even the greatest criminal once was.

Matthew's version of the judgment of the world is not meant to devalue this. I think it's a good thing that God wants to realize his justice in co-operation with human beings who are neither purely sheep nor purely goats. I think it's a good thing that he has others helped by people who are no angels but have both good and bad in them. And I hope that one day, when all that is left of us is simply what we are in God's judgment, this judgment as a whole will nevertheless be a positive one.

This Bible study was given in Munich on 11 June 1993 at the Kirchentag of the Evangelical Church in Germany. The modern myth of justice which is compared with Matt.25.31-46 is to be found in J.Rawls, *A Theory of Justice*, Oxford University Press 1971, esp. 159ff.

Jesus and Hippocrates

The end of anxiety about demons

(Mark 9.14-29)

When they came to the disciples, they saw a great crowd around them, and some scribes arguing with them. When the whole crowd saw him, they were immediately overcome with awe, and they ran forward to greet him. He asked them, 'What are you arguing about with them?' Someone from the crowd answered him, 'Teacher, I brought you my son; he has a spirit that makes him unable to speak; and whenever it seizes him, it dashes him down; and he foams and grinds his teeth and becomes rigid; and I asked your disciples to cast it out, but they could not do so.' He answered them, 'You faithless generation, how much longer must I be among you? How much longer must I put up with you? Bring him to me.' And they brought the boy to him. When the spirit saw him, immediately it convulsed the boy, and he fell on the ground and rolled about, foaming at the mouth. Jesus asked the father, 'How long has this been happening to him?', and he said, 'From childhood. It has often cast him into the fire and into the water, to destroy him; but if you are able to do anything, have pity on us and help us.' Jesus said to him, 'If you are able! – All things can be done for the one who believes.' Immediately the father of the child cried out, 'I believe; help my unbelief.' When Jesus saw that a crowd came running together, he rebuked the unclean spirit, saying to it, 'You spirit that keeps this boy from speaking and hearing, I command you, come out of him, and never enter him again!' After crying out and convulsing him terribly, it came out, and the boy was like a corpse, so that most of them said, 'He is dead!' But Jesus took him by the hand and lifted him up, and he was able to stand. When he had entered the house, his disciples asked him privately, 'Why could we not cast it out?' He said to them, 'This kind can come out only through prayer.'

My wife spent six months in Bethel living with epileptics. When I was about to prepare this Bible study on the healing of the epileptic boy, she said: 'There are still prejudices against epileptics. People still don't know that epilepsy is a disease like any other. It is not hereditary. It is not a mental illness. It doesn't necessarily lead to mental handicap. And it is quite certainly not demonic possession, as is presupposed in this story.'

Nevertheless epileptics are still discriminated against in our society, for example in appointments to public service. Enlightenment is still necessary.

The story of this enlightenment begins in antiquity. Around 400 BCE an unknown physician whose writing has been preserved under the name of Hippocrates (and for the sake of simplicity I shall call him 'Hippocrates') composed a work on epilepsy, the 'sacred disease', as it was called in his time. His revolutionary theory was that epilepsy is a normal illness. It is not caused by the gods and so it is not a 'sacred disease'. Its origin lies in the brain, and it can be cured. His view became established only in modern times, in the face of great obstacles. The story of the epileptic boy was one of these obstacles. The church father Origen commented on it with the words: 'Doctors may ... seek a natural explanation (for the disease), since in their view no unclean spirit is at work here but there is a manifestation of the disease of the body... but we also believe with the Gospel that this sickness... is brought about by an unclean, dumb and deaf spirit' (on Matt.13.6). Such judgments had an influence.

This story still caused difficulties for Friedrich von Bodelschwingh, who founded the institutions at Bethel. For love of his sick patients he had to defend them against the view that epilepsy derived from the working of Satan and was no ordinary illness.

We have to concede that at first glance a deep abyss opens up between the enlightened view of Hippocrates and the biblical belief in demons. Can it be bridged? Are the two traditions perhaps complementary? Do they both belong together – as rationality and mercy, enlightenment and love belong together?

Both after all seek to help sick people.

As a first step I want to discover the specific associations the narrators of the biblical miracle stories had with demons and how they countered them.

Then I want to tell two other stories from the time of Jesus about the driving out of demons in order to show what belief in demons implied at that time.

As a third step I then want to point out a timeless element in anxiety about demons and argue that we need both Hippocrates and Jesus to cope with this timeless background to the fear of demons.

I

First, let's ask, 'What in particular is understood to be the action of the demon in this story?' There are two features which are not necessarily connected with epilepsy, namely dumbness and self-inflicted hurt.

The demon is introduced as a 'spirit that makes him unable to speak' (v.17) and later as a 'spirit which keeps the boy from speaking and hearing' (v.25). This does not just mean that the boy is incapacitated during an attack. For he is also dumb between the attacks. That is the only explanation why he does not make the request, but his father asks for him. We would say that he has a multiple handicap.

A second time it is said of the demon that it hurls the boy into fire and water to destroy him. Here too we have associations with the experience that epileptics can have fatal falls – of course, also into water and fire. But that is not a specific tendency of this disease. Rather, this story is about extreme self-inflicted hurt: auto-aggression, if not a suicidal tendency.

The father's additional statement that the boy has had all this from childhood (v.21) also fits epilepsy. In antiquity it was called the 'child's suffering' *(puerilis passio)*. But further experiences also seem to have found their way into the description of the sickness – say, with autistic children who do not speak and display aggressive behaviour against themselves.

The decisive thing for us is that at that time many people beyond question regarded an epileptic attack as the work of a demon. However, this hostility was shown for the narrator of Mark 9 less in the picture of the sickness itself than in these two tendencies of an inability to communicate and self-inflicted hurt, which go beyond the symptoms of usual epilepsy. The narrators of this story sensed that the threat was not the epilepsy in itself but the social isolation to which it led. Inability to communicate and self-inflicted hurt – all this strengthened their impression that such people were not in control of themselves. An uncanny, alien, hostile power had seized them. This power drove them towards death. The demon tugs the boy to and fro and leaves him with a loud cry. His cry could be the first sign that the demon has been overcome: hitherto it had been a dumb spirit. But even on capitulating the demon seeks to harm the boy: the boy falls to the ground. The people say, 'He's dead.' But Jesus takes him by the hand and helps him to stand up. The word can also be translated 'and he raised him'. The conclusion is narrated like a raising from the dead, and this may be deliberate: the conflict of the demon is meant to be depicted as a conflict with a deadly power, as a battle between the power of death and the power of life.

The evangelist Mark has deliberately given the story this form. For elsewhere in his Gospel demons are associated with death and killing. In the great exorcism of demons by the sea of Galilee (Mark 5.1ff.), the demons drive those who are possessed to live in caves. They seem to be near death. That is made even clearer by the end of the story: the demons, who call themselves 'Legion', enter into a herd of swine and drive them into the sea, where the animals drown wretchedly. These demons, too, drive their victims 'into the water'. The collective suicide of the swine that they cause shows that the demons are hostile to all life, and not just to human life.

So we need to note that for the narrator of this story, the 'demon' is a power which kills by an inability to communicate and by self-inflicted hurt, a power which is hostile to life.

Let's now go on to ask: what is set against the effect of this demon? The story gives a clear answer: the power set against the demon is faith. It is mentioned three times.

The first time, unbelief is mentioned. When the father tells Jesus of the vain attempt by the disciples to heal his son, Jesus answers with the lament, 'You faithless generation, how much longer must I be among you? How much longer must I put up with you?' (v.19). This unbelief will first be referred to the disciples. They have failed. What Jesus means is that if they had more faith they would have been able to heal the sick boy. But as a rule, the world 'generation' denotes all the people in a generation or a nation. In that case, in our story it would also include the father, who in fact later confesses his incomplete faith. It would also mean the sick boy with his suicidal tendencies. It would also include the scribes who in an earlier version of the story had perhaps once ventured exorcism, but had failed. At all events, here 'unbelief' is a general characteristic of human existence. When Jesus complains about it, he means more than the lack of a capacity to heal. It is as if he wanted to say, 'Were there more faith everywhere, i.e. more power among people which furthered life and brought healing, then such self-destructive tendencies which break off communication could not prove as destructive as they do with this child.'

The second time, the father speaks of faith in a quite remarkable way. He has asked Jesus, 'If you are able to do anything, have pity on us and help us.' What Jesus in effect says in reply is, 'You are saying to me "If you are able to do anything" (and you are doubting my power), but I am telling you that the one who believes can do anything.' This phrase, 'the one who believes can do anything', transfers a divine predicate to human beings. God is the one who can do anything (cf. Mark.10.27; 14.36). If the same thing is said of faith, it means that just as unbelief is a characteristic of human existence generally, so faith is an expression of divine existence. First of all the reference is to Jesus. He is the 'one who believes', who has a share in the power of God. He was able to say: 'But

131

if it is by the Spirit of God (the finger of God) that I cast out demons, then the kingdom of God has come to you' (Matt.12.28; cf. Luke 11.20). That means that God himself is active in Jesus' power of exorcism. But the saying 'the one who believes can do anything' equally clearly applies to the father. For he takes up this promise when he says, 'I believe, help my unbelief.' He wants to have a share in this omnipotent faith.

As we saw, for the narrators of the story demonic power is a self-destructive drive leading to death, whereas faith is an unconditional will to life. God himself is this unconditional will to life. To believe means to have a share in God's will to life and make life possible through it.

The third time, there is a mention neither of unbelief nor of unbelief, but of both. The father confesses, 'I believe, help my unbelief.' His confession of unbelief can be understood specifically as a reaction to Jesus' promise of omnipotent faith: must not all human beings shrink back from attributing divine omnipotence to themselves? Sometimes we have these fantasies of omnipotence. When we meet people who inflict hurt on themselves and cannot communicate, then our being cries out, 'If only we had a bit of divine power to make life possible for these people! If only we had God's power to put hopelessly splintered people together again! Or even the power to remove the suffering of a single child!' But such fantasies of omnipotence are born of despair. In them we go beyond ourselves. They do not lead to help for others but only to a helper syndrome in ourselves in which we ask far too much of ourselves. The evangelist Mark warns against this. He gives the disciples some special instructions in the house: this kind of demonic power, he tells them, cannot be conquered by normal means. Only God himself can conquer it. So you must pray for the sick.

Thus in our story faith is spoken of in three ways:

1. All human beings live in 'unbelief'; all human beings lack unconditional trust in life. Here unbelief is a characteristic of human existence.

2. Faith is omnipotent. That makes it a divine power. Here

faith appears as an expression of the existence of God.

3. The father has both belief and unbelief at the same time. The split between human unbelief and the divine omnipotence of faith runs right down the middle of him.

In the light of this whole story we can now say that its special feature is the contrast between faith and the demon, between the power of life and the power of death. This contrast is also unusual as a narrative form: the motive of faith occurs elsewhere only in healing stories without demons – as confidence in the great miracle worker. It is remarkable that here faith is included in a story about demons. It is strange that faith is so clearly understood as a force which counters the demonic!

As a second stage, we must now find out more precisely what people of that time were afraid of when they trembled before demons and what they found to be the liberating power of faith. To show that, I shall quote two further stories about the driving out of demons: a Jewish story and a pagan story from the first century CE.

II

In the Jewish historian Josephus we find the report of the expulsion of a demon which took place during the Jewish War (c.67/68 CE). Josephus either saw this himself or had a reliable report of it. For he mentions a series of witnesses, some of whom were still alive when he wrote down the story between twenty and twenty-five years later. In other words, there must be something to the story. This is what he says:

'I have seen (or experienced) how one from our people, a certain Eleazar, in the presence of Vespasian, his sons, the military tribunes, and a crowd of other soldiers freed those possessed of demons. The healing took place like this. He put to the nose of the person possessed a ring under whose seal had been placed one of the roots which Solomon had indicated (for this purpose). When the man had smelt it, he blew the demon out through his nostrils. The man immediately collapsed and Eleazar conjured the demon never to return to him again. In so doing he mentioned the name of Solomon and performed the incantations that Solomon had composed. And to show those present that he really had this power, he set a vessel or a trough in front of him and commanded the demon to knock it over when he came out of the person, thus indicating to the onlookers that he had left the man. And so it happened...' (Josephus, *Antiquities* 8,45-9 = VII, 2, 5).

Two differences between this exorcism and the miracles of Jesus should be emphasized.

The first is that Eleazar works with magical means and traditional knowledge which was attributed to king Solomon: the ring and the root correspond to Solomon's recipes, and Solomon's name and incantations banish the demon. Eleazar heals in the power of another authority. In the story about Jesus, faith and faith alone takes the place of all these means: the faith of the miracle-worker and the faith of those who seek his help. We find no magical knowledge, no tradition, no great authority of the past, but only this faith. Here time and again it is fascinating that when people stream to Jesus to be healed they seek the great miracle-worker who can do what they cannot. But Jesus contradicts this expectation. He points them to themselves. His saying 'Your faith has saved you' gives the person seeking help a share in the healing. Something in them was at work in the healing, their faith in Jesus and God. This faith is also referred to in the story of the epileptic boy. It is the faith of Jesus and of the father who seeks help. This faith is the real cause of the healing. Through it, human beings become the subjects rather than the objects of health and healing.

The second difference is that Eleazar conjures the demon never to return to him again. He does not destroy it, but only drives it out. The Gospel of Mark differs. In the first of the three great exorcisms in the synagogue at Capernaum the demons cry out to Jesus, 'What have we to do with you, Jesus of Nazareth? You have come to destroy us.' Jesus does not just drive the demons out, banish them to another place, ward them off – so that they can continue to do their dirty work elsewhere. According to the Gospel of Mark, he destroys them. That is his mission. That is what he has come for. And the demons know it. The kingdom of God which dawns with Jesus is a world without demons. That is even how it is defined. 'But if it is by the Spirit of God that I cast out demons, then the kingdom of God has come to you' (Matt.12.28). Then the whole demonic rule with Beelzebul, the chief of the demons at its head, collapses. That is what the so-called Beelzebul saying says (Mark 3.22ff.).

But as well as these two differences there is also a positive point of contact between Eleazar and Jesus. Eleazar performs his exorcism in the presence of the general Vespasian and his sons – i.e. the later imperial family of the Flavians, who were there to put down the Jewish revolt and to subdue the land. The story of Eleazar's exorcism will have been told with great satisfaction in Jewish circles at that time. It shows that while Vespasian had the power to subdue Palestine, when it came to subduing demonic forces, the Jewish king Solomon had the greater power.

By contrast, for Christians Jesus of Nazareth had the superior power. His miracles were regarded as more powerful than all rival miracles – so powerful that at the end of the Gospel of Mark even the representative of the world power, a Roman centurion, recognizes the greatness of the crucified Jesus, 'Truly, this man was God's Son' (Mark 15.39). The demons whom Jesus drives out also have to do with this world power. One of these demons proudly calls himself 'Legion', as though he were a division of the Roman army. He wants to remain in the land like the Romans. But he is driven into the sea – something that many people in Palestine would have liked to do to the Romans. These demons are the representatives of oppressive alien powers. Their supreme ruler is called Beelzebul. This name must have made anyone in Syria and Palestine think of the numerous Baal gods in and around Palestine. When Jesus drives out not only individual demons but the ruler of the whole demonic band – some Baal deity who was a demon in the eyes of the Jews – it is clear that anxiety about demons is also anxiety about superior political and cultural power. Power over demons means resistance to them and liberation from them. In other words, where there is a situation of political oppression and cultural threat, belief in demons flourishes. It expresses an awareness of being threatened from outside. An analogy can make that clear. In Siberia, ethnologists observed a tribe which was dominated by the neighbouring tribe. Those in the tribe that was dominated who were possessed spoke the language of their dominators. This prompts the following reflection on our story. In it the demon is called an 'unclean spirit'. In the eyes of the Jewish population anything pagan, alien, associated with idolatry was unclean. That in addition it is called a deaf and dumb demon points to the pagan gods, since according to Jewish belief they can neither speak nor hear (cf. Pss.115.4-11; 135.15-18; Isa.44.20). They, too, were deaf and dumb. And for Jews, foreign gods were demons.

We can derive an important insight from the social and historical context of belief in demons in New Testament Palestine. In working as an exorcist, Jesus relieved ordinary people not only of their individual anxiety about the threat from sickness, but also of their collective anxiety about the threat from foreigners – from Romans, Syrians and Greeks, from their uncleanness and idolatry, their military and cultural power. In so doing he created the presuppositions for them to become open to aliens. For that can happen only when one has overcome anxiety about what is alien in oneself.

So we cannot make a sharp distinction in Jesus between an 'enlightened' openness to the alien on the one hand and the primitive exorcisms on the other. For the awareness that demonic powers have already finally been conquered and are on the retreat everywhere created the presupposition for openness to aliens. But the power for overcoming the demonic was the faith that gives a share in God's power, in God's will for life.

Now it would be quite wrong as a result to regard the capacity for exorcism as intrinsically already a progressive feature. On the contrary, it can have the opposite effect: it can be destructive and prejudicial. That is what I want to illustrate with my second story, which also takes place in the first century CE. It tells how the Neo-Pythagorean philosopher Apollonius of Tyana combated an epidemic in the city of Ephesus. He gathered the youth of the city together in the theatre, where an old beggar was sitting, and called on them to stone him. At first the younger people refused. They thought it inhuman to stone a stranger, especially one who was pleading for his life. But Apollonius went on at them. Some began to throw stones. Then the beggar looked at his tormentors. They thought they could see fire in his gaze – the evil eye. It was clear that he was a demon. Thereupon they shed all their inhibitions. They stoned him. The story ends like this:

'After a little while Apollonius had the stones removed in order to look at the being that they had killed. When the stones were put aside, the man seemed to have disappeared. In his place they found a dog, in form and likeness resembling the Molossus (i.e. a kind of wolfhound), as big as a lion. He had been completely shattered by the stones and was foaming like a mad beast' (*Life of Apollonius* IV, 10).

Even if this story is legendary, it is certain that something like this could have happened. Foreigners and outsiders were said to be demonic, and collective aggression was unleashed against them in order to cope with crisis in the community. Anyone can recognize the mechanisms which help to form prejudice here: aggression born out of anxiety is directed against a scapegoat who is sacrificed for the well-being of the community. Belief in demons gives a slender justification to anxiety about the threat of witches, ghosts and demons – and has often had this effect in history.

That is why it is so important to make clear the difference between the driving out of demons by Jesus (and charismatic healers akin to him) and this kind of fight against demons. In the story of the demon in Apollonius, the man is identified with

137

the demon. The fight against the demon is aggression against the man in whom the demon is supposed to be. But in the other stories about the driving out of demons the sick person is distinct from his demon. The human person is saved and healed when the demon leaves him.

Despite this difference, in one respect both stories of demons (those involving Eleazar and Apollonius) teach the same lesson: belief in demons always has a social and political context. It reflects a feeling of collective threat: threat from an alien political power or an epidemic. Exorcisms and stories of exorcists serve to reduce this anxiety. The decisive thing is the way in which they take action against the anxiety. Is it by killing people who, it is thought, can be identified as the cause of the collective anxiety, in which case we end up with witch and demon crazes? Or is it by liberating people from the claws of the demon so that in the exorcism the power of life prevails against death? The decisive difference between a humane and an inhumane culture does not lie in whether there is belief in demons in it or not. If that were the difference, we would have to regard most cultures and societies as inhumane. Most societies believe in demons and spirits. The decisive thing is whether the battle against demons heals people or destroys them. The New Testament knows only a healing fight against demons.

III

In this last section I want to take our analysis one stage further: the anxiety which is fought against in exorcisms has an even deeper level – beyond all political and social contexts. It is rooted in archaic prehistory and is a universal human heritage that we only overcome gradually in the course of cultural evolution. Here we have the archaic double anxiety about uncontrollable enemies in our environment, and about loss of control over ourselves.

The story of Apollonius reveals something to us about the origin of the first form of anxiety about demons: the demon is unmasked as a dog or a wolf, a monster as big as a lion. The anxiety about demons is rooted in those times when people were still directly threatened by animals and were helpless when faced with them. We have in us an archaic proneness to anxiety from that prehistory, which can constantly be activated. Even enlightened contemporaries can feel this anxiety when going alone through a wood at night, when there are noises in the bushes and the tops of the trees rustle in an uncanny way. Then we are back in the jungle, in which we cannot see the predators, but they can see us. Anyone can then understand what the fear of ghosts and demons is: it is the projection of nocturnal predators to which we are exposed defencelessly in the jungle (thus K.Lorenz).

And whenever life is experienced as jungle, as a dangerous chaos which we can no longer master, then this primal anxiety will revive in us (often unconsciously). It turns into anxiety about invisibly present enemies – demons, witches, conspirators and so on. This connection between the archaic fear of beasts and the fear of demons is also clear from the fact that many demons in antiquity have the names of animals.

Most cultures know a second form of anxiety about demons, the fear of being possessed, the fear that a demon will enter into a person and take that person over to the same degree as a driver who is banished to the back seat and has to look on helplessly while another steers the vehicle into the abyss. Such anxiety about being possessed appears particularly in cultures which also know positive ecstatic states of being outside oneself. Such positive and negative states, which people are now seeking to understand in terms of neuro-physiology, seem to be an opening for processes of alienation and repression in which self-control is lost to destructive tendencies, so that it used to be said, 'He is possessed'. The deviant state of consciousness so to speak 'goes off the rails'. Most pre-modern cultures can now control or produce such states of being outside oneself and can stop or put an end to such instances of going off the rails. 'Exorcists', shamans and medicine men are the experts here. And I have no doubt that Jesus had such exorcistic capacities –

i.e. the capacity to stop people 'going off the rails'. Anxiety about this kind of behaviour (i.e. being possessed by a demon) has tormented all cultures before us in a way that we find difficult to understand.

Both forms of fear of demons are thus deeply rooted in archaic times, when people had only limited control over the environment and lived in constant fear of losing control over themselves. There is the anxiety about the 'beast' in the jungle – and anxiety about the beast in us. These archaic anxieties must go right back to the transitional period between animal and human being. Forms of reaction and possibilities of experience acquired at that time are still unconsciously present in all of us. So we cannot conquer them simply by declaring that there are no demons. Indeed there aren't – at least that is what I think. But the archaic anxiety in us continues to exist. It's real. And we shall have to go on coping with it in the future. Here we have two allies, Jesus and Hippocrates.

At first that may seem amazing. Isn't Jesus himself an exorcist? Didn't he share in a painful way the belief in demons of his time? And wasn't Hippocrates an opponent of those who wanted to attribute diseases like epilepsy to demons? All that is true. Nevertheless, Jesus and Hippocrates have things in common.

Hippocrates wanted so to speak to drive 'belief in demons' out of people's heads as an explanation for epilepsy. By contrast, Jesus wanted to drive the demons themselves out of the world. One fought against wrong ideas, the other against the realities to which these ideas related. However, in the final result both these fights really aim at the same result: whether we removed belief in demons from our heads or the demons from the world, the result would be a world free of demons, a world without anxiety about demons.

Of course we could follow many modern men and women in saying that Hippocrates and his enlightenment are far more important than Jesus' struggle for a world free of demons. For it is quite logical that if one is convinced that there are no demons, one needn't bother driving them out.

Now it is doubtless important to join Hippocrates in driving out belief in demons from peoples' heads. But that isn't enough. Why not? Here are two reasons.

First, human beings are not just head and cerebrum. In human beings there are archaic levels which still continue to believe in demons, even if our understanding is convinced that they do not exist. It is not enough to destroy wrong ideas, for what lies behind them must similarly be transformed. Now behind the demons lurk our archaic anxieties. So even now, we need the images of the Jesus who drove out demons so that we can conquer these anxieties, so that we become free of the fear of demons, right down to the deepest levels of our unconscious. There is a small child who is afraid of demons in all of us. This child will not grow up simply by being told that there are no demons. It will grow up through faith, through faith that we have God as an ally in the battle against everything that harms life, through faith that participates in God's unconditional will for life, through faith by which God himself is present in us.

This small child in us which is still afraid of ghosts and demons needs support from Jesus above all in one respect: it is afraid of the consequences of its own misconduct. If it does something bad, it thinks that it will be tormented by evil spirits. We find this anxiety in many cultures, and in some people in our society even today.

There is no trace of that in the exorcisms that are related of Jesus. Those possessed are poor people. The epileptic boy has not committed any sin, nor has his father. If anything, all have failed him: the totally unbelieving generation, everyone. But there can be no question of those possessed being tormented by their demons as punishment for past guilt. In a sentence, the moral judgment on people who are deeply disturbed, in a way which was called possession at that time, is abolished. 'Don't moralize, help' is the slogan. And here Jesus agrees with Hippocrates. Hippocrates speaks out against treating those with epilepsy as though they had committed a crime and therefore had to be kept away from the temples. Precisely the opposite must be done: 'Pray, bring the patients to the temples

141

and appeal to the gods' (*De morbo sacro* 1).

Now for the second reason why Jesus is our ally in the fight against our archaic fear of demons. One could indeed say that he held views which we regard as obsolete, because he applied the term 'demon possession' to the 'derailments' which take place in the brain in deviant states of consciousness, which have not yet been fully researched. We tend to regard that as a time-conditioned interpretation of deep psychological disturbances. But in one respect Jesus presents a view which leads beyond Hippocrates in the direction of the truth. Let me recall it: of all the exorcists of antiquity (and perhaps even of the whole world), Jesus is the only one who says, 'My work has basically put an end to the rule of demons. With my work the rule of God is coming. There will be no more demons in it.' In other words, Jesus interprets the overcoming of demons and the fear of demons as a decisive step beyond the whole of previous history. He sees in the end of the demons the coming of the rule of God here and now. A new phase of reality is already beginning now. By contrast, for Hippocrates, as for all Greeks, reality was static, defined by the recurrence of the same. That it is in principle moving towards a new state was an idea which first emerged in the biblical tradition.

In fact I believe that the overcoming of the archaic anxiety about demons in us represents a step into a new world: in so far as we are afraid of being overcome by the environment around us or by alien impulses within us, we constantly remain at the stage of biological evolution in which we are deeply rooted. Only when we overcome anxiety about the loss of control of an obscure environment and of ourselves, panic anxiety about the 'beast' in the world and the unleashing of the 'beast in us', are we really the first free beings in creation.

To repeat the point once again: to take this step we need both Hippocrates and Jesus as allies. Hippocrates embodies the rationality of the physician. This tells us that we can explain and heal diseases and disturbances. By contrast, Jesus embodies the mercy that motivates us to care even for those who are hopelessly ill and see the help given to them specifically as small steps into the kingdom of God. He embodies faith as an unconditional will to life. Rationality and mercy, enlightenment and love, belong together.

But it has taken a long time for them to come together. Despite Hippocrates, for centuries epilepsy and many other diseases were attributed to demons. Despite Jesus, Christians usually did not believe that his appearance had finally put an end to the demons. Rather, they created unthinkable suffering as a result of demon- and witch-crazes. Neither tradition could establish itself because the collective and individual anxieties about threats were too great not to keep provoking anxiety about demons. Only in modern times – on the basis of the Enlightenment – has it been possible for a culture to come into being in which anxiety about demons has been 'banished' from wide areas, even if there have been, and constantly will be, waves in which the archaic anxieties about demons arise. But they can be banished by enlightenment and love. They can be combated where rationality and mercy join forces. They can be overcome where both reason and love serve an unconditional will to life. I at any rate would dread a society and a church in which the two were not allied. I would dread a world which had lost the knowledge that both love and reason are committed to saying an unconditional Yes to life, namely to God himself. But the two have in fact already come together. In the last century they joined forces in Bethel, where today we have the greatest medical centre in the country for treating and researching into epilepsy. Both Hippocrates and Jesus would have been delighted at that.

This Bible study was given in Bochum at the Kirchentag of the German Evangelical Church in the Ruhr on 6 June 1991.

'You aren't rubbish, you're seeds!'

My grandmother's wisdom

(Luke 8.4-8)

When a great crowd gathered and people from town after town came to him, he said in a parable: 'A sower went out to sow his seed; and as he sowed, some fell on the path and was trampled on, and the birds of the air ate it up. Some fell on the rock; and as it grew up, it withered for lack of moisture. Some fell among thorns, and the thorns grew with it and choked it. Some fell into good soil, and when it grew, it produced a hundredfold.' As he said this, he called out, 'Let anyone with ears to hear listen!'

Only a few parables in the Gospels are given an explanation. One of them is the parable of the sower and his seed. At a very early stage it was found so enigmatic that hearers were not expected to understand it without guidance. The image of the seed was a familiar one. That was precisely why everyone understood something different by it.

Some probably thought, 'We're the seed. God has cast us into the world to bear fruit.'

Others thought, 'The seed is our actions, in the sense of Paul's admonition, "What a person sows (i.e. does), he will reap."'

Yet others perhaps thought, 'The seed is God's word, which is scattered everywhere but rarely comes to anything.'

The parable is ambiguous. No exegete today can decide between the three interpretations without making an arbitrary choice. But this very ambiguity is an opportunity; it makes it

144

easy to hear the parable as it is meant to be understood: as an invitation to discover in reality something that corresponds to it, as poetry for a journey of discovery into life.

The first interpretation says, 'We're the seed! We aren't stones, we aren't rubbish, we aren't nothing. We're seed which is meant to bring forth fruit.'

How good it must feel to be conscious of being fruitful! Of being *worth* something. But how tormenting doubts about this are! They are almost unavoidable if one grows up in a strict Reformed community. That was already made clear to me as a child, 'You aren't thrown into this world to wangle your way though it somehow. You're seed which is meant to produce fruit, even if there are obstacles and there is much barren ground. I remember rough and ready pastors who fulminated against the idea of the 'dear God'. God wasn't a 'dear God', they exclaimed, but a God of love. But this love always seemed to me to be a harsh pedagogical love: an education in reality with the aim of losing all illusions about oneself and the world: that was the only way in which one could be effectively fruitful. That was what one had been chosen for. That was one's task. That was the message.

It caused me anxiety as a child. Was I one of those who were of some use? Was I perhaps one of those who had fallen – by the wayside, on the rocks, among the thistles? Who were these lost seeds? Were they the children who never did their homework and always had grubby exercise books? Were they the seedy looking men who always had a bottle of beer in their pockets? Were they all those of whom my grandmother said in her broad accent, 'It's God's will that these people should also be alive.' And if one asked, 'Then why do things go so badly for them?' she would only say, 'The worst suffering is what people inflict on themselves.' And that put God in the right – a least for my grandmother.

She really didn't have things very easy. She had a husband confined to a wheelchair, and four grandchildren whose home had been bombed: their mother had died and their father was in a prisoner-of-war camp. She and another daughter looked after them. She had experienced great loss. And how did she cope with it all? With the daily Bible reading texts, and time and again with, 'The worst suffering is what people inflict on themselves.'

How many people I've met since then have felt that they were wasted seeds – cast on a hostile world in which they could find no roots, no room, only cold rocks and thistles! There are the desperate who say, 'I've never succeeded in anything. I'm always sitting in the dark.'

There are those who have been abandoned and doubt whether they are worth anything to other people.

There are the suicidal people who are dragged down by a seductive voice – into a deadly silence in which all suffering will come to an end.

And in addition, at present there are the voices of those who come to us only indirectly, hidden from the television pictures in which we see only the 'smart bombs' exploding, but almost never the far smarter people who are torn to pieces and destroyed by them. How many children do they include? How many will lose their parents? And not all of them will find a grandmother to bring them up.

These voices of the lost hold our attention – and so we can hardly hear the message of the parable. For what it says is, 'No matter how many are lost, some, a few, will produce all the more fruit.'

One feels like protesting against this message. Even in antiquity at the end of the first century a Jew protested against the identification of seeds and people. He complained to God, 'How can you identify human beings, your image, for the sake of whom you have created everything, with seeds which quickly perish if they get rain too early or too late?' And rather later, a Christian Gnostic thought that the parable of the sower must speak of an evil God, and of an incompetent farmer who loses the seed.

And what about us? Can we quietly take our place among these critics? I can't explain why so many in our world are lost.

Nor do I want to. I refuse to look for an explanation. For we only magnify the suffering of those who are lost if we tell them, 'Not only are things in fact going badly for you, but there is a good reason why, indeed it's what you deserve.'

Perhaps the parable gives us an indication of how we could be thinking. 'They are all good seeds. None is a stone, none is rubbish or worthless. They are all destined to bear fruit. No seed is deliberately thrown aside.'

We are told quite specifically that the sower went out to sow, not to throw things on one side. He wants success. Failure happens contrary to his will. We are all good seed. And when I meet those who are lost, I tell myself that the same seed is in them as is in me; they are programmed to live as I am. However, it was impossible for them to develop – in conditions in which I, too, would have been crippled. There is no higher purpose behind this. Unfortunately creation is constructed in such a way that this sort of thing is possible. Perhaps it hasn't been completed. But once one has been converted to reality, there is no point in denying that in the world there is barren land. However, nowhere is there the task of making it barren – by bombs, poison and desolation. That was not intended.

Nevertheless, everything remains a cruel game. We cannot deny it, but we shouldn't be content with it.

That brings me to the second interpretation of the parable. The seed is our actions. We are the sower. What a positive effect the parable now has on me! Isn't it true that our actions often go astray? How often we get bogged down! How often our actions shatter on the stony reality and how many plans get stifled in the thorns of life!

And what about you? How much land is barren in you? How much in you has been trodden down by footprints, made stony by suffering, overgrown by weeds and thistles?

Don't be discouraged! Somewhere there is good ground, around you and in you. One day, somewhere, your seed will fall on fertile land, however much failure you had previously. Somewhere, some day, you will blossom and produce much fruit.

When I had left the Reformed piety of my childhood years and become a child of the world like everyone else, it dawned on me that this world is constructed in such a way that every success must involve failure. There is no knowledge without error, no economy without bankruptcy, no growing up without crises, no life without sickness. There is nothing without losses; everything has its price. But if by your actions you take part in this game of winning and losing, then you too have become a player in this reality. No matter who has constructed it, no matter what you know and believe about him, your relationship to the unknown constructor is that of an image: delighting in risks, wanting success, but taking involuntary failure into account.

Science is our most successful attempt at taking part in this game of winning and losing. It teaches us to prefer false hypotheses about the statics of buildings to collapse, rather than the buildings themselves. It kills off our hypotheses so that we survive. It makes our errors fall on the path, on the rocks and among the thistles, so that the truth compensates us a hundredfold.

One can play this scientific game of winning and losing and repress and forget God. In that case, at least there is no need to reflect on why God allows so many to be lost. But whether one likes it or not, one is always playing God's game, according to rules which none of us has devised, which we found already in existence and which we can only accept.

Once you have become aware of this and it dawns on you (though you are a child of the world like everyone else) that you are not alone in this game, then you may appear before the one who has imposed such a harsh education in reality on you and say:

'God, you've constructed this creation in such a way that there is no loss without gain. That's hard. Nevertheless, I will join in your game. For you have given me a unique opportunity, to co-operate so that fewer people are lost. All you ask of me is voluntarily to lose something of myself, of my power, my time, my life – so that I may get it back thirty, sixty and one hundred fold. Your creation is harsh. It has a defect. But it is not yet finally built. You have created us to overcome this harshness. And by taking part in your game of creation and being confident that it can be humanized, we justify it so that we can assent to it – not least through our protest against its harshness.'

In my youth I thought like that for a long time. And basically I still think in the same way today. But my education in reality had not yet been completed. Once again I had to spell out my grandmother's wisdom, 'The worst suffering is what people inflict on themselves.'

For what is worst is the illusions that we have about ourselves.

That brings me to the third interpretation of the parable. The seed, that is the word. That is God's call, which is addressed to you, though you are as hard as rock and as resistant as thistles. This word robs you of your illusions about yourselves.

It says, 'You are right. You should see that people aren't lost. But are you doing that? Aren't you doing the opposite?'

'What are you doing in science? Just experiments which make life possible? Aren't you building terrible weapons which threaten all life, which today are threatening Israel – and thus once again your moral integrity?'

'What is your economy producing? Only goods which make life possible? Aren't you also above all producing dependence on prosperity, a dependence which drives us to wars when we see this prosperity threatened?' Our society is addicted – addicted to oil, with all the destructive consequences of a life-threatening addiction.

'And what are you doing with religion?' Certainly it has become a great motive force in the longing for peace. But it is caught up in the fanaticisms which threaten to destroy our world. Conflicts seem especially insoluble wherever religion is involved, in India, Pakistan, Northern Ireland, the Middle East.

'That's what human beings are,' says God's call . 'That's what you are. And do you want to repair the ugly defect in creation, to prevent so many people from being lost? Do you want to justify creation by your action? You fool, don't you see how much yourself need to be justified by the Word of God.'

And this Word tells you: 'You have failed in the task of humanizing creation. Nevertheless God holds fast to you. God condemns your actions but not your persons. He marks down your failure as loss but puts you yourself on the profit side. He makes a distinction between person and work.'

This message of justification has the same structure as a humane scientific ethic. That says that you may reject hypotheses so that you yourself may survive. The message of justification says, 'You may reject all your actions so that you yourself are not rejected. You may live.'

The humanity of this message of justification as it is to be found in Paul and Luther was a great discovery for me, once I had left the house of my childhood piety and got to know the land of secular awareness. This message is more humane than science, more favourable to life than prosperity, more tolerant than religious fanaticisms.

We need to listen to it today. Who knows how many words and deeds we perpetrate which will be intolerable in days to come – because they have brought the world nearer to the abyss. And that applies to all of us. It applies to those who affirm the Gulf War as the ultimate reason for preventing the worst, the worst of all. And it applies to those who see it as wicked playing with fire among the oil tanks of the earth. The hour is coming for us all when we have to say, 'Forgive us our trespasses, as we forgive those who trespass against us.'

So I understand my grandmother's wisdom today once again in a new way – as a comfort: people are responsible for what they do to themselves. This need not be. It's their fault. But whoever is to blame can also be forgiven – and vice versa. And where people are converted, the world can become different.

We've run through three variations of the parable.

We are the seed. God has cast us into the world. There is a risk that many will perish. Hence, fortunately, the second interpretation.

The seed is the actions with which we can help the lost. However, we fail and often increase the losses. So it is a good thing that there is also the last interpretation.

The seed is God's word which sets us upright when we fail and leads us to repentance.

However, all three variations keep the sinister fact that something is lost. Even God's Word is lost. It doesn't reach everyone for whom it could be vitally important to detect something of the love of God. So I must add another, last, variation. In the Gospel of John the image of the seed is applied to Jesus himself. There we read:

'Unless a grain of wheat falls into the ground and dies, it remains alone, but if it dies, it bears much fruit.'

Here Jesus himself is the seed that dies. He himself is lost. So let's read the parable of the sower yet again:

A sower went out to sow. But among the seed there was a grain of corn with which he particularly identified. This particular grain of corn was lost. It fell on the hard path, it shrivelled up on the rocks, and was stifled among thistles. It died in the earth in order by its death to bring forth much fruit: thirty-, sixty- and one hundredfold.

What does that mean? It means that the rough and ready pastors of my childhood were right. God is not the 'dear God' who rules everything so splendidly. There is no guarantee that everything that we plan and do here will go well. In this world, something of God gets lost. God is a God of love who in the one human being, in Jesus of Nazareth, his Son and our brother, has put himself on the side of all who are lost.

When I was a child, I was terrified by the message that we are the seed, destined to be fruitful. Who knew whether they were fertile land?

When I grew up, I recognized that God is present in those who think that they are barren land, worthless and useless. God is not only among those who go their fixed way, who stand out like rocks in the crises of life and can find a place for themselves in the jungle of existence.

God is among those who know that there is often no

justification for what they do and have done.

God is among those who long to be created anew, because they detest the way in which they are entangled in uselessness and inhumanity.

God is among those who hunger and thirst for righteousness, because they do not possess it.

Today I can understand afresh what my grandmother's saying 'The worst suffering is what people inflict on themselves' means. The worst thing is for people to stifle in themselves the belief that they are fertile seeds. The worst thing is for people to shut themselves off from the love of God. That love comes to us anonymously in any friendliness, in any help, any laughter and any embrace. It comes to us directly through God's Word. That Word keeps telling us: 'You're seed. Even if you're having a rotten time. Even if grief has turned you to stone. If that has happened, it is even more the case that you are not rubbish. You aren't stones. You're miraculous seed in God's hand.' Amen.

This sermon was given in St Peter's Church, Heidelberg, on 3 March 1991, eighteen days after the outbreak of the Gulf War. The Jewish author from the end of the first century CE mentioned in the sermon is the author of IV Ezra. He makes Ezra say in a dialogue with an angel who brings revelation, 'For if the farmer's seed does not come up, because it has not received your rain in due season, or if it has been ruined by too much rain, it perishes. But man, who has been formed by your hands and is called your own image because he is made by you, and for whose sake you have formed all things – have you also made him like the farmer's seed? No, O Lord, who are over us! But spare your people and have mercy on your inheritance for you have mercy on your own creation' (IV Ezra 8.43-45), in J.Charlesworth (ed.), The Old Testament Apocrypha, I, Darton, Longman and Todd and Doubleday 1983, 543. A Gnostic writing Memoria Apostolorum (quoted in Orosius, a second-century writer, 154, 4-18) says that the sower of Matt.13.3ff./Luke 8.4ff. was not a good sower. It comments that 'had he been a good sower he would not have been neglectful and would not have cast any seed either "by the wayside" or "on stony places" or have scattered it in "untilled soil"'. The author is talking about the imperfect and evil god of this world (cf. W.Schneemelcher [ed.], New Testament Apocrypha I, Gospels, Westminster/John Knox Press and James Clarke 1991, 376).

Worshipping God in Spirit and in Truth

The mysticism of the Gospel of John and the dialogue of the religions

(John 4.1–41)

Now when Jesus learned that the Pharisees had heard, 'Jesus is making and baptizing more disciples than John' – though it was not Jesus himself but his disciples who baptized – he left Judaea and started back to Galilee. But he had to go through Samaria. So he came to a Samaritan city called Sychar, near the plot of ground that Jacob had given to his son Joseph. Jacob's well was there, and Jesus, tired out by his journey, was sitting by the well. It was about noon.

A Samaritan woman came to draw water, and Jesus said to her, 'Give me a drink.' (His disciples had gone to the city to buy food.) The Samaritan woman said to him, 'How is it that you, a Jew, ask a drink of me, a woman of Samaria?' (Jews do not share things in common with Samaritans.) Jesus answered her, 'If you knew the gift of God, and who it is that is saying to you, "Give me a drink," you would have asked him, and he would have given you living water.' The woman said to him, 'Sir, you have no bucket, and the well is deep. Where do you get that living water? Are you greater than our ancestor Jacob who gave us the well, and with his sons and his flocks drank from it?'

Jesus said to her, 'Everyone who drinks of this water will be thirsty again, but those who drink of the water that I will give them will never be thirsty. The water that I will give will become in them a spring of water gushing up to eternal life.' The woman said to him,

'Sir, give me this water, so that I may never be thirsty or have to keep coming here to draw water.' Jesus said to her, 'Go, call your husband, and come back.' The woman answered him, 'I have no husband.' Jesus said to her, 'You are right in saying "I have no husband"; for you have had five husbands, and the one you have now is not your husband. What you have said is true!' The woman said to him, 'Sir, I see that you are a prophet. Our ancestors worshipped on this mountain, but you say that the place where people must worship is in Jerusalem.' Jesus said to her, 'Woman, believe me, the hour is coming when you will worship the Father neither on this mountain nor in Jerusalem. You worship what you do not know; we worship what we know, for salvation is from the Jews. But the hour is coming, and is now here, when the true worshippers will worship the Father in spirit and truth, for the Father seeks such as these to worship him. God is spirit, and those who worship him must worship in spirit and truth.' The woman said to him, 'I know that Messiah is coming' (who is called Christ). 'When he comes, he will proclaim all things to us.' Jesus said to he, 'I am he, the one who is speaking to you.'

Just then his disciples came. They were astonished that he was speaking with a woman, but no one said, 'What do you want?' or, 'Why are you speaking with her?' Then the woman left her water jar and went back to the city. She said to the people, 'Come and see a man who told me everything I have ever done. He cannot be the Messiah, can he?' They left the city and were on their way to him.

Meanwhile the disciples were urging him, 'Rabbi, eat something.' But he said to them, 'I have food to eat that you do not know about.' So the disciples said to one another, 'Surely no one has brought him something to eat?' Jesus said to them, 'My food is to do the will of him who sent me and to complete his work. Do you not say, "Four months more, then comes the harvest?"? But I tell you, look around you, and see how the fields are ripe for harvesting. The reaper is already receiving wages and is gathering fruit for eternal life, so that sower and reaper may rejoice together. For here the saying holds true, "One sows and another reaps." I sent you to reap that for which you did not labour. Others have laboured, and you have entered into their labour.'

Many Samaritans from that city believed in him because of the woman's testimony, 'He told me everything I have ever done.' So when the Samaritans came to him, they asked him to stay with them;

and he stayed there two days. And many more believed because of his word.

'In dialogue between religions and confessions people often fail to make real contact. But there is one exception: if one brings together the mystics from all religions and confessions, they immediately understand one another.' This remark by a specialist in religion keeps going through my head when I read the story of the Samaritan woman at the well. This story, too, tells of a dialogue between different religious groups, between Jews and Samaritans. They too failed to make real contact, indeed they were entangled in hatred and enmity, although they believed in the same God, had a long history in common and shared the five books of Moses as Holy Scripture. And in our story, too, the bond between them is created by a mystical spirituality, by the recognition that God is spirit and must be worshipped in spirit and in truth, independently of rival places of worship, independently of the temple in Jerusalem or the sacred Mount Gerizim, independently of Rome or Mecca, independently of Moscow or Washington. The narrative breathes the spirit of Johannine mysticism, the experience of a new union between God and human beings through the spirit. Here such 'mysticism' overcomes the barriers between religions and confessions.

That comes about on the level of human relations through a woman. That too is no chance. Women often overcome barriers in the New Testament. In the Gospel of Mark the Syro-Phoenician woman is the first of all Gentiles to have contact with Jesus. In Acts, Lydia, who trades in purple, is the first Christian from all the Greeks. In the Gospel of John, Jesus first reveals himself to the Samaritan woman with the word of revelation 'I am'. She is the first to bear the message beyond the bounds of Judaism.

Finally, the overcoming of social barriers takes place at yet a third level: by the exchange of material things. Jesus and his disciples need water and food. So they have to make contact with Samaritans. That is why Jews and Samaritans are dependent on one another in the story.

To understand the inner drama in this story we must first envisage the barriers between Jews and Samaritans. Here we are looking at a history of prejudice and aggression. Some features recall the relationship between Protestants and Catholics in Northern Ireland or between Turks and Greeks on Cyprus. As a second step, against the background of such tensions we shall read the story of the Samaritan woman by the well again – as an encounter between Jesus and a woman, as an exchange of material things, and as imagery which discloses a mystical experience. Here we shall ask what the sublime Johannine spirituality, which is often remote from the world, has to do with the harsh social reality of this world.

So first some historical information about the relationship between Jews and Samaritans.

Contrary to a tenacious prejudice, the religious division between Jews and Samaritans does not go back to Old Testament times. Certainly we keep coming across political tensions between the northern kingdom and the southern kingdom and later between Samaritans and Jews, but they shared the same faith. Only at the end of the fourth century BCE, when Alexander the Great's campaigns of conquest created new political conditions throughout the Near East, did some Samaritans take the opportunity to built a sanctuary of their own on Mount Gerizim (cf. Josephus, *Antiquities* 11, 321-4). They told how Abraham had been received hospitably by Melchizedek on this mountain (cf. Gen.14.17-24). So they worshipped God on it (cf. Eusebius, *Praeparatio Evangelii* 9, 15, 5). This foundation story of the Samaritan sanctuary shows how highly the Samaritans rated hospitality towards strangers. We can also recognize this from the fact that a reform movement among the Samaritans in the second century wanted to give the God of the Bible whom they worshipped a name which was also comprehensible to Greeks, the 'hospitable Zeus', Zeus Xenios. These reforms aimed at worship of God which no longer marked itself sharply off from the Greeks and from aliens.

At the same time there were similar attempts at reform

among the Jews in Jerusalem. Their supporters no longer wanted to cut themselves off from all other peoples; they wanted to change in order to overcome what in their eyes was the pernicious segregation of their own people and their own religion from all others. So the Jerusalem reformers called God 'Zeus Olympios'. Their slogan was, 'Let us go and make a covenant with the Gentiles around us, for since we separated from them many disasters have come upon us' (I Macc.1.11). They were opposed by the rebellion of the country fundamentalists, the Maccabean struggle. For the latter, the very existence of a second temple on Gerizim was an abomination, let alone the identification of the God of the Bible with Zeus. As soon as they had achieved political independence and sufficient military power, they destroyed the capital and the temple of the Samaritans (128 or 107 BCE) – probably in the hope of reversing the religious split by the forcible integration of the Samaritans.

But that didn't happen. Although they no longer had a temple, the Samaritans did not come to the Jerusalem temple. They kept to their separate form of biblical faith. In so doing they led possibly one of the greatest revolutions in religious history: they were probably the first to practise a religion not only without a temple cult but also without the majority of the traditional bloody animal sacrifices. Of all the sacrifices that the Old Testament knows, to the present day they celebrate only the Passover sacrifice on Mount Gerizim. It could be that they have never performed the other sacrifices since the destruction of their temple. They worshipped God above all by liturgies of the word. Jews and Christians later followed them here, at the latest after the temple in Jerusalem had also been destroyed in 70 CE. In short, the Samaritans took a first step on the way towards worshipping God 'in spirit and in truth', in the direction of worship of God without bloody sacrifices.

But the tensions between Jews and Samaritans continued. The Jews looked down on the 'foolish people of Shechem' (Sirach 50.25f.). They insinuated that the Samaritans were foolish because they knew nothing of the God whom they worshipped – a derogatory judgment which the Johannine Jesus also takes over (John 4.22). Perhaps the Samaritans in fact claimed that God was above all understanding – so that he could be worshipped even without a temple and the usual sacrifices. God was quite different from the way in which we understand him. So they were waiting for a prophet who in future would bring enlightenment about the true worship of God. The prejudice against them twisted this into the insinuation that the Samaritans themselves conceded that they did not know what they worshipped. This was reason enough to avoid contact with such people: 'Jews do not share things in common with Samaritans,' as the Samaritan woman remarks (John 4.9).

Some interludes in the first century CE illustrate this tense relationship:

Interlude 1. Hardly had the Romans taken over the direct administration of Judaea and Samaria in 6 CE than some Samaritans perpetrated a macabre attack on the Jerusalem temple. While all the people of Jerusalem were in their homes eating the Passover meal on Passover night, these Samaritans crept into the temple and scattered human bones in it. This desecrated the temple (Josephus, *Antiquities* 18, 29-30; *Jewish War* 2, 117). We can agree that such provocations against other forms of religion are certainly not worshipping God in 'spirit and in truth'.

Interlude 2. Under Pilate, a Samaritan prophet attracted a group of followers and went with them to Mount Gerizim to show them the missing temple vessels which according to Samaritan tradition Moses had buried there. Had they found them on Gerizim, this would have been understood as an indication from God that God wanted to be worshipped here and not in Jerusalem. But Pilate intervened brutally and had the crowd of people massacred. The uproar over this massacre led to his deposition in 36 CE (Josephus, *Antiquities* 18, 85-89). Incidentally, we should recall that this Pilate had already given a Galilean prophet short shrift. This prophet, too, had prophesied a new temple – only not on Gerizim, but in Jerusalem.

Interlude 3. This took place in the fifties. When crossing

Samaria on the way to Jerusalem, a Galilean pilgrim was murdered. This was the spark which set off the powder keg. Samaritan and Galilean 'bandits' (we would call them terrorists) plunged the land into a serious crisis (*Antiquities* 20,118ff.). The Roman historian Tacitus speaks of outright war (*Annals*, 12.45). Here, too, I might recall that the hostility of Samaritans towards pilgrims on their way to Jerusalem is well known from the New Testament. According to the Gospel of Luke (9.51-56) Jesus is not welcomed in a Samaritan village because he is on the way to Jerusalem. Two of his disciples want to call down fire and brimstone from heaven upon the village, i.e. commit arson with divine help. Jesus sharply rebukes them. The narrative is a good illustration of the hostility on both sides – and that although the Samaritans rated traditional help and hospitality highly. It was the same old story. All peoples have humane ideals, including us. But when it comes to unpopular aliens and neighbours, these ideals tend to be suspended.

The three interludes have one common factor: they all involve the rivalry between two sanctuaries and confessions. Religious convictions overlie an earlier political conflict and make it virtually insoluble. The story of the Samaritan woman by the well sets against this rough reality the utopia of worshipping God in spirit and in truth! It counters it with the sublime notions of Johannine mysticism. It counters hatred and prejudice with enigmatic images of water and food.

If we are to understand the gentle protest of this story against the harsh reality of prejudice and aggression, we need to read it on three levels:
– First on the level of relationships: Jesus encounters a woman.
– Secondly on the material level: Jesus receives water and food from others.
– Thirdly on the level of symbolism: 'water' and 'food' become images of a mystical experience.

(*a*) In our first reading of the story we shall concentrate on the relationship between Jesus and the woman. Those who know their Bibles will recall the idyllic scene by the well when a bride is being sought for Isaac. This Old Testament story gives the New Testament scene by the well a kind of background eroticism. Most interpreters of the Bible do not dare to say this openly – any more than do the disciples, who after their return from the place in Samaria find Jesus in an intense conversation with a woman by the well. They merely discuss it among themselves. They are offended. No wonder! For the narrative presupposes that both Jesus and the Samaritan woman are setting themselves above origins and culture in making contact with each other – a Jewish man and a Samaritan woman. That inevitably confuses the disciples. But they don't dare to ask openly what Jesus has to do with the woman. It is as if they don't want to ask Jesus any embarrassing questions. However, readers can answer their unspoken question, since previously they have read the dialogue about the marriages of the Samaritan woman, over which there has been much puzzling. They know that Jesus has previously touched on the topic of marriage and sexuality on his own initiative. He does not do so in order to expose the woman as a loose-living slut. Nowhere do we find any indication of criticism of the woman's life-style. She has had an extraordinary life. She has had five husbands. They have either died or separated from her by divorce. But she is not formally married to her present partner. Jesus accepts her extraordinary life. He respects the woman's human ties, including her non-marital tie to her present partner. (Just a little sigh in passing: if only all Christians could accept the extra-marital relations of their fellow men and women in the way that Jesus does in this story!). However, for the story itself it is important that the woman's initial statement, 'I have no husband', at her meeting with Jesus by the well, is still somewhat ambiguous. It could give readers with experience of well scenes the impression that a tender interlude is being prepared for. But when Jesus himself exposes the woman's relationship to a man and acknowledges this relationship by saying, 'You've spoken well,' for the reader he rules out any background eroticism which is involuntarily associated with scenes by a well. Now it is clear that Jesus does not want to flirt. He wants to encounter the woman as Revealer. He wants to encounter her as the expected Messiah who will teach how God is to be worshipped in Spirit and in truth. He says his 'I am' for the first time to this woman, even before he reveals himself in his great 'I am' sayings: I am the bread of life, the light of the world, the good shepherd; I am the resurrection and the life; I am the way, the truth and the life; I am the vine. Jesus reveals the truth first to a woman – in a scene by a well which involuntarily evokes thoughts of the sexual roles of man and woman. Against this background the story says that God is worshipped in spirit and in truth where man and woman grow beyond their sexual rules and overcome the barriers of communication imposed on them by custom and origin. So the scene by the well becomes a place of revelation – a place where man and woman meet, but here in a more sublime sense, namely in the worship of God in spirit and in truth.

(*b*) Before we turn to the question of what is meant by this worship in spirit and in truth, we must read the story a second time: in a 'materialistic' and concrete way. For every now and then the Gospel of John in particular, for all its sublime mystical spirituality, gives us surprising glimpses of the harsh facts of this world.

So it can be no coincidence that the course of the story is determined by the most basic of all material questions – the question where we get water and food from. The woman gives the water; the disciples get the food from the village. In neither case is it simply there.

Nor can it be fortuitous that in this story Jesus appears as someone in need. He asks for water. He needs bread. Others bring it to him.

Finally, it can be no coincidence that the story speaks of the human work which goes into the provision of such vital commodities: the work of the woman who has to go to the well in the heat of the day to draw water, and the work of sowers and harvesters which is presupposed in every slice of bread. Water and bread are not just there. They only become available through human work. They are laboriously created.

But one thing above all becomes clear: like all food, water

and bread are scarce. No unlimited supply is at our disposal. Water has constantly to be drawn, bread constantly worked for. Those who drink and eat will thirst and hunger again.

Religion occurs for the first time in this context: it is the basis for the right to the possession of these scarce material commodities. The well is Jacob's well. 'He gave it to us' says the Samaritan woman (John 4.12). Jacob legitimates their possession of it down to the present. Wells safeguard opportunities for living. The Old Testament knows them not only as idyllic places for initiating marriages but also as places which are fought over (cf. Gen.21.22-34). The right to them must be justified, established and defended. That happens on the one hand with physical force and on the other with religious tradition – with an appeal to the patriarch Jacob, to whom this well once belonged and who bequeathed it to the Samaritans for all time.

Granted, all these are trivialities. And yet they are tremendously important. This sublime Johannine story in particular shows something of the harsh fight for the distribution of scarce material opportunities in life. And it shows that religious traditions are often merely the background music which gives people a good conscience in this fight over the distribution of commodities.

One thing is unmistakable in our story. As long as the Samaritan woman is moving on the level of material commodities and the legitimation of them by religious traditions, she fails to understand Jesus. When Jesus speaks of living water', he does not mean the well. Jesus does not mean Jacob when he speaks of the one who gives this water of life. The Samaritan falls into a typical 'Johannine misunderstanding', as the disciples do later.

We find this misunderstanding not only in the Gospel of John but also in the whole history of Christianity and the religions. Religion is time and again misused to legitimate the distribution of opportunities in life and to fog the fight for the distribution of scarce material commodities. This misuse of religion must constantly be opposed. That is why I am disturbed by the slogan 'Marx is dead, Jesus is alive'. Marx analysed the struggle over the distribution of material commodities. He often got it wrong. And indeed Marx is dead. But the struggles over distribution that he analysed are not. They still continue. And we must not tolerate such ongoing struggles over distribution between East and West, North and South. Faith in Jesus must not be the meditative and mystical background music to the noise of the struggles over distribution in our society. That would not be worshipping God in spirit and in truth. For this worshipping God in spirit and in truth points beyond the struggle over opportunities in life. But how?

(*c*) To discover that, we need to read the narrative a third time. In the Gospel of John events and words have a symbolic meaning in addition to their literal sense. So too here. Water is the symbol for an energy which bestows eternal and true life. Jesus gives this energy. Jesus says: 'Everyone who drinks of this water will be thirsty again, but those who drink of the water that I will give them will never be thirsty. The water that I will give will become in them a spring of water gushing up to eternal life' (4.13f.). Here we have a play on the ambiguity of the term 'living water'. In Greek it primarily means water from a spring – as opposed to water in cisterns and wells. But the evangelist understands the expression in a symbolic sense: by 'living water', Jesus means a 'life-giving force'. Here he is thinking of the spirit. For in John 7 he speaks once again of 'living water'. There Jesus says of the believer: 'From his heart will flow rivers of living water.' And the evangelist explicitly adds an interpretation: 'Now he said this about the spirit, which believers in him were to receive' (John 7.38f.). So Jesus is promising the Samaritan woman the spirit of God, an inexhaustible source of the power of life. He is promising her something which makes true worship of God possible – an inner harmony with God. For God himself is spirit – and true worship of God takes place through the spirit. It becomes possible because the 'spirit of God', i.e. God himself, is present and active in his worshippers. It takes place in those who possess the spirit and are thus in harmony with God who is himself spirit. It happens through those who are one in being with him. If that is not 'mysticism', I don't know what mysticism is. Even if 'mysticism' is one of the bad words of twentieth-century Protestant theology, we shouldn't avoid it. There has been mysticism in Christianity time and again, and not just in the late Middle Ages. We find it also in our church hymns, in Paul Gerhardt and Gerhard Tersteegen. And beyond question there is also mysticism in the New Testament, above all in the Johannine writings. But this is mysticism of a special kind. What distinguishes it? I shall now attempt to work out three characteristics of this Johannine mysticism.

The first characteristic follows from the twofold image of water and food. Just as water has a symbolic significance, so too does food. When the disciples come to Jesus and bring him food, Jesus says, 'I have food to eat that you do not know about... My food is to do the will of him who sent me and to complete his work' (John 4.32, 34). Here the 'food' becomes the symbol for God's will. This will is to be done. And it is to be assimilated by human beings just as much as outward food. So Johannine mysticism is in the first place a mysticism of the will, a union of the will of God with the human will. It is less a mysticism of enjoying, of vision, of the peak emotional experiences than a mysticism of doing. I John contains the central statement of this Johannine mysticism of the will and of love: 'God is love, and those who abide in love abide in God, and God abides in them' (I John 4.16).

The second characteristic of Johannine mysticism follows from the contrast between literal and symbolic meaning. Water and bread (in the literal sense) are limited. They have to be shared. The more people have a share in them, the smaller the portion that each receives. But there is no limit to the availability of water and bread in the symbolic sense. The spirit of God, God's will, God's love, do not become any the less by the fact that many people are seized by them. Those who get their share are not consuming anything that others lack. They are not taking anything away from anyone. Rather, these spiritual commodities gain all the more value, the more people share in them. Here there are no struggles over the distribution of scarce commodities. On the contrary, if people become open to God's reality, they enter a sphere which lies beyond all struggles over distribution. That has repercussions on the earthly struggle over distribution. Once someone has discovered that the real commodities can be distributed at will, he or she will also share the material commodities with others. I John puts it like this: 'How does God's love abide in anyone who has the world's goods and sees a brother or sister in need and yet refuses help?' (I John 3.17). That is why it is so important that we should read this narrative not only on the symbolic level but also on the material level. The dividing line between Jews and Samaritans is broken through on both levels. Everything begins on the material level. The specific beginning of everything is that at the request of Jesus a Samaritan woman gives him water to drink. Sharing 'in the spirit and in truth' begins with the sharing of earthly commodities; it begins with eating and drinking.

We can infer yet a third characteristic of Johannine mysticism from the story. Jesus does not just say to the Samaritan woman, 'I am giving you living water. I am the source. Draw from it as long as you want.' Rather, he says, 'The water that I give you will become a source in *you*. *You* will become someone who receives the energy of life rather than someone who expends energy; you will become a source rather than a vessel; one who gives abundantly rather than one who is lacking.' In fact the Samaritan woman does not remain passive. She changes from being a recipient of the word to one who hands on the message. It is striking that a similar statement is made in the dialogue between Jesus and the disciples. Jesus says that his food is the will of God; he wants to complete his work. He compares this work with the sowing and harvesting on the fields around. The one who sows is not the one who reaps. Here Jesus is referring to the sorry fact that there are always those who have worked only to have others profit from their labour. However, the work of doing the will of God is different. Here, 'The reaper is already receiving wages and is gathering fruit for eternal life, so that sower and reaper may rejoice together' (John 4.36). Here there is no division between those who have laboured and those who have had the results. Here no one profits at the expense of anyone else. Just as with the image of the spring of life the contrast between the recipient and the giver is done away with, so with the image of the bread the contrast between workers and reapers is overcome. While the two are not identical, both rejoice together.

In the two images of water and bread we recognize an important characteristic of Johannine mysticism. Dependents are to become independent, subordinates are to become equals, slaves are to become friends (John 15.15). We are all dependent on the fortuitous religious traditions in which we have grown up. We are dependent on parents and teachers. Like the Samaritans, we are dependent on the traditions of Judaism. For in Judaism for the first time the idea of the one and only God became established; the commandment to love was formulated in Judaism, and Jesus and his disciples came from Judaism. Salvation is of the Jews (John 4.22). We enter into their work, and profit from their toil, their suffering, their experience. But where God is worshipped in spirit and in truth we grow out of dependence on our own traditions and encounter God in an original way. Through God's spirit we are no longer vessels but a spring, no longer recipients but givers, no longer objects of the message but its subject. We appropriate what we have received as tradition in a new and original way – as if we ourselves had discovered it. The story makes this clear in a very simple way. The Samaritan woman runs to her city and proclaims Jesus there. Through her many people come to believe – independently of the tradition which is handed down through her. But then the Samaritans who have thus come to believe meet Jesus himself. And they say to the woman, 'It is no longer because of what you said that we believe, for we have heard for ourselves, and we know that this is truly the saviour of the world' (John 4.42).

Let me mention briefly once again the three characteristics of Johannine mysticism:

1. It is a mysticism of the will – becoming one with the love of God. It is not an individualistic mysticism, but a social mysticism. Worship of God 'in spirit and in truth' takes place only where it results in connections with other people – even beyond the abysses of prejudice and hatred.

2. It is a mysticism which seeks to limit and overcome the struggle over the distribution of scarce commodities. It seeks to get beyond the dispute between rival wills for life – trusting in an inexhaustible wealth of spiritual commodities. Whether God is worshipped 'in spirit and in truth' is shown by a reduction in the struggle over the distribution of material opportunities in life.

3. It is a mysticism which seeks to liberate people from their dependence on religious tradition by leading them from second-hand encounters with God to first-hand encounter. We worship God 'in spirit and in truth' only where we gain inner freedom from our traditions; where we ourselves experience what they bear witness to.

Does what I said at the beginning, that the mystics in all religions can very quickly reach an agreement, whereas the dogmatic theologians fail to make contact, fit this Johannine mysticism? Some doubts are not out of place. To make them clear, I must define rather more closely the type of religion that we find in the Gospel of John.

In principle it is possible to distinguish between two types of religion, a mystical type and a prophetic or kerygmatic type. The ultimate reality and the world in which we live is different for both. Just as every animal lives in its particular environment, so too does the human being. Just as we can ask what the ant knows of the sun, so we can ask what human beings know of the ultimate reality which underlies everything. But there is one difference. Human beings know that the world in which we live is not identical with reality in itself. Human beings are aware of the limits of the world in which they live. And they ask how they can make contact with this ultimate reality.

In the kerygmatic religions, contact is made by a message

which comes from outside. Kerygma means' message'. God confronts people by addressing them from outside through events and messages. By contrast, the way of mysticism is a way inwards. It is taken in the hope of encountering God at a deep level of the self, remote from our normal consciousness.

The two types of religion can be combined. The Western religions – Judaism, Christianity and Islam – are by their basic structure kerygmatic religions. But everywhere there is a mystical counter-current in them. The Eastern religions, Hinduism and Buddhism, are mystical religions. But they also have prophetic-kerygmatic movements.

In its basic structure, beyond question the Gospel of John belongs to the kerygmatic type of religion. God makes himself known in it by a call from outside human beings. There is a deep gulf between God and human beings, as there is between light and darkness, truth and lie, life and death. Jesus comes from beyond this gulf as the emissary of the Father. In the Gospel of John he makes an unprecedented claim, 'I am the way, the truth and the life. No one comes to the Father except through me' (John 14.6). This is where the problem lies. Don't such statements close the door to dialogue between the religions? Doesn't the Gospel of John bear the blame for the excesses of the Christian claim to absoluteness? Doesn't it at least share the blame for the long history of Christian anti-Judaism, a hostility to Jews who did not want to take this one way to the truth and to life? Aren't the Jews already branded 'children of the devil' in an intolerable way in the Gospel of John (cf. John 8.44)?

I concede that these questions have tormented me for a long time. It often seems to me as if the Gospel of John has two sides: a warm, tolerant, mystical side, and another side, which is cold, intolerant and dogmatic. But it would not be a good thing to end a Bible study with tormenting questions.

However, that is not the only reason why I want to give you my answer to these questions. Here it is important to recognize that the Gospel of John is a unique combination of the kerygmatic and the mystical types of religion: human beings do not just receive the message from a radical Beyond. Rather, they are changed by this message and themselves become the embodiment of it. The will with which they are confronted from outside is combined with their own will within.

The decisive thing now is, 'What kind of a will is that?' 'For what is the claim to absoluteness made?' It would be one-sided to say that in the Gospel of John this claim is made for Jesus himself. Rather, the Johannine Jesus says, 'Whoever believes in me believes not in me but in him who sent me' (12.44). The sending of Jesus, his task, is the decisive thing. Time and again in the Gospel of John, Jesus says that he has been sent by the Father. That he brings a message. But time and again people puzzle over what his message really is. Often it seems that his message is above all that he is the messenger. Indeed one could think that in the Gospel of John the Revealer reveals only that he is the Revealer. But that is quite manifestly a statement without content. That cannot be all. Now in the farewell discourses Jesus finally unveils his message. Here he says emphatically that he is now telling all his disciples what he has heard from the Father, so that from now on they are no longer slaves, but friends; no longer dependants but equals. For the son of a householder tells only friends what his father has said, not slaves. This message is clear. It runs:

'This is my commandment, that you love one another as I have loved you. No one has greater love than this, to lay down one's life for one's friends. You are my friends if you do what I command you. I do not call you slaves any longer, because the slave does not know what his master is doing; but I have called you friends, because I have made known to you everything that I have heard from my Father' (John 15.12–15).

With this, Jesus has said it all. The love commandment is everything: in it he has stated the only way to the Father, the only truth, the way to life. It is love. The claim to absoluteness in the Gospel of John is an absolute claim of love. It is the way, the truth and the life. No one comes to the Father but by it. Jesus is only the way, the truth and the life because he is the messenger of this love. To believe in him means not to believe in him but in the one who has sent him, in God. Now God himself is explicitly defined three times in the Johannine writings: as spirit (John 4.24), as light (I John 1.5) and as love (I John 4.16). And time and again it is said that human beings are destined to have a share in God's being: God is spirit, and wills to be worshipped in spirit and in truth. God is light, and wills that people should live in light. God is love. And those who love, abide in God and God abides in them. That is the core of Johannine mysticism.

If we Christians take part in the dialogue of religions and suffer from its difficulties – the many claims to absoluteness that we find in our traditions; the struggles over distribution with which the conflict of the religions is indissolubly associated; the growing struggles over distribution between East and West, North and South – then we should make sure that we smuggle a Johannine mystic into this dialogue behind the backs of the dogmatic theologians (including the Johannine dogmatic theologians). Perhaps this mystic will make one of the most important contributions to the dialogue of religions, to a worship of God in spirit and truth that brings everyone together. For the Samaritans, this way to the true worship of God at that time meant the beginning of a gradual end to bloody animal sacrifices. Christians, Jews and Muslims followed them further here. But a decisive step was taken only in modern times, after the Enlightenment, a step which has still not ended: the decisive thing is to put an end to the bloody human sacrifices made in the wars of religion and the heresy trials of religious which have been the consequence of claims to absoluteness. Worshipping God in spirit and truth will not have been achieved until it is clear everywhere that there is only one claim to absoluteness, that of love. We must measure everything critically by it – including our own religion, the New Testament, Protestantism. Those who do not begin by measuring themselves against this claim have no right to measure others by it. Those who do not gain inner independence from their particular traditions cannot require it of others. Even the worship of God in spirit and in truth will always be governed by particular traditions – among us, Jewish, Christian and humanist traditions. But that does not mean that we should absolutize these traditions. Only God is absolute, and not the traditions which bear witness to him. Only God is the truth itself, not the images that we produce of God. Only God is the ultimate reality, not the temples in which we worship him, whether these be in Jerusalem or on Gerizim, in Rome or Wittenberg, in Mecca or Benares, in Washington or Moscow. For the worship of God in spirit and truth will only have reached its goal where each individual becomes the temple of God, in which God's spirit, God's light and God's love dwell – and where no one goes under in the fight over the distribution of opportunities in life.

This Bible study was given on 8 June 1991 in Bochum at the Kirchentag of the German Evangelical Church in the Ruhr and on 13 October 1991 in Versailles.

The Dream of a Life that does not Live at the Cost of Other Life

(Romans 5.8)

But God proves his love for us in that while we were still sinners Christ died for us.

This morning we shall be reflecting on this week's saying from the Bible. Many people find it offensive that Paul thinks that God shows people his love through the death of an innocent person. They ask, 'Did God need to do that? Couldn't God have shown his love in another way? Isn't God acting cruelly and unjustly in delivering his own Son over to death? Is the Bible inhuman in one of its central ideas?'

People will always have difficulty with the image of the vicarious death of Christ. I too did – until I came to see that the problem which causes offence lies even deeper: it is not that God makes someone die a vicarious death but that we constantly make other life die for us – not just once, but time and again. Not only in archaic, prehistoric times, but to a heightened degree in the present.

Here I am thinking first of all of the many creatures which have fallen victim to the expansion of *homo sapiens* – not only the unimaginable number of individuals but the countless species whose genetic information has been excluded for ever from the process of the world. A zoologist told me that he would begin his lectures by saying that during the course of the lecture series their subject-matter would decline substantially.

We are living in a time when an unimaginable number of species are dying out. Why? Because our form of life is imposing itself at the expense of others.

Archaic societies knew something of this connection. They knew that life lives at the expense of other life. For centuries, at the centre of religion there were bloody sacrifices, acts of killing in which people slaughtered animals in the hope of being able to protect and enhance their own lives. We have no right to feel superior to such archaic societies. We sacrifice animals to a gigantic extent – to expand and enhance our own lives.

In the light of that we would have to say, 'God shows his love in that Christ has died for us, just as we sacrifice yet other living creatures for us.'

Unfortunately, however, things do not stop with the sacrifice of animals. We also make people die for us. There is a connection between the wretchedness of underdeveloped states and our prosperity. The fact that elsewhere life-expectation is around forty years, whereas among us it is around seventy, means that the early deaths of others contribute to the average age to which we live.

Now it might be objected that these are very indirect connections. We do not sacrifice any human beings. We have got beyond this archaic stage. Other societies may have even sacrificed their children – we don't.

But are we so sure? Don't we sacrifice the lives of our children directly and indirectly in a way that goes beyond anything perpetrated by previous generations?

We live more intensively at the cost of future generations than anyone ever has done in the history of humankind so far. We are destroying the foundations of their lives by exploiting the resources of the environment and negligently endangering them. Nor is that all. We are even ready to sacrifice the life of our children directly. Here I'm thinking of the many abortions. To avoid any misunderstanding, let me say that I am incapable of blaming anyone who has an abortion. For me, too, the loving care of parents for a new-born child is part of human life – a life which is repudiated is a dead life, a life overshadowed by the refusal of love. Nevertheless, I think that for us every abortion is a defeat – a defeat for the will to life. I am sad at the large number of abortions and feel deep moral uncertainty as to whether this is a good thing. The large number of future lives which have been killed holds up a mirror in front of us: in a terrifying way we are ready to sacrifice the life of our children to save our own lives; to protect them, if not enhance them.

So our saying for the week ought to run: 'God shows his love in that Christ died for us, just as we make other people die for us.'

Wherever I look, people are living at the cost of other life. Everywhere we are living at the cost of other life: the life of animals, of the people next to us, of unborn life. We are all entangled in a pernicious web. No one is free. No one is without sin. For this pernicious web is sin – it is a lack of love, an offence against that which binds all life together.

Once we have become clear what is really scandalous and depressing, namely that human beings let other life suffer in their place, then we can understand the image of the vicarious dying of Christ in a new way.

Through the image something of the love of God can dawn on us.

God himself enters the world in which life lives at the expense of other life. In Christ, God is near to all human beings who have to suffer for others. In Christ God shows that he suffers because of this world, where the large fish devour the little fish. In this world God shows his love in that Christ has died for us, so he is near to us in this world in which life dies for another life.

But more than that, God shows an alternative to this world. God provides a model for a contrary practice. God shows that love consists in not sacrificing other life for oneself but sacrificing one's own life for others or, more modestly, in sacrificing something of one's own life so that others have something of it. So we can say, 'God shows his love in that Christ died for us so that we may become free from the compulsion to make other life die for us.'

This is how the first Christians understood it. Because Christ brought all that people had hoped for from sacrifices, they put an end to bloody sacrifices. They refrained from actions associated with the shedding of blood. Certainly they said that a soldier might become a Christian (provided that as far as possible he refrained from bloodshed), but they would hardly have said that a Christian should become a soldier. At any rate they had strong scruples about this. They rejected posts in which people shed blood. They thought that fights between gladiators were bad.

We must learn in an even more comprehensive sense what it means that in Christ a life has appeared which does not live at the expense of other life. This is a life which is no longer subject to the laws of this world, in which all life seeks advantages at the expense of other life. This is a life in which a new world begins – in the midst of the old.

It begins when we sense the power to sacrifice something of our own lives so that all the creatures on this planet can live with us. It begins when we find the power to limit some of the possibilities for our own life so that our children can also live on this earth.

It begins when we become free from the compulsion to sacrifice other life for ourselves. It begins in our hearts when we feel the peace of God which passes all our understanding. May that keep our hearts and minds in Christ Jesus. Amen.

This sermon was given at the Wednesday morning service at St Peter's Church, Heidelberg in March 1990.

Is Paul's Criticism of the Law Anti-Jewish?

(Romans 9.1-5; 9.30–10.4)

I am speaking the truth in Christ – I am not Lying: my conscience confirms it by the Holy Spirit – I have great sorrow and unceasing anguish in my heart. For I could wish that I myself were accursed and cut off from Christ for the sake of my own people, my kindred according to the flesh. They are Israelites, and to them belong the adoption, the glory, the covenants, the giving of the law, the worship and the promises; to them belong the patriarchs, and from them, according to the flesh, comes the Messiah, who is over all, God blessed for ever. Amen.

What then are we to say? Gentiles, who did not strive for righteousness, have attained it, that is, righteousness through faith; but Israel, who did strive for the righteousness that is based on the law, did not succeed in fulfilling the law. Why not? Because they did not strive for it on the basis of faith, but as if it were based on works. They have stumbled over the stumbling stone, as it is written, 'See, I am laying in Zion a stone that will make people stumble, a rock that will make them fall, and whoever believes in him will not be put to shame.' Brothers and sisters, my heart's desire and prayer to God for them is that they may be saved. I can testify that they have a zeal for God, but it is not enlightened. For, being ignorant of the righteousness that comes from God, and seeking to establish their own, they have not submitted to God's righteousness. For Christ is the end of the law so that there may be righteousness for everyone who believes.

All the texts for this Sunday are about Israel's catastrophes and Israel's greatness. Including this one. On the one hand Paul is proud of his Jewishness, of the presence of God in the history of Israel; on the other hand he complains that most Jews reject belief in Jesus – for Paul an incomprehensible catastrophe, a failure on the part of Israel. Paul mourns over Israel and hopes for its renewal through Christian faith. He is divided, and so are we, but in a different way from him. We lament that Christianity has failed Israel, and hope that it will be renewed from its Jewish roots. Such mourning and hope make the text eerie, precisely because it contains a fascinating image and a grandiose idea.

First of all the image. Life is a race. All human beings are on the way to a goal, namely to accord with God. Paul calls this goal the righteousness of God. Jews are most obviously competing for it. The Gentiles do not even seem to have started. But then an uncanny feature enters into this picture. God appears as a trapper. He puts an obstacle in the way, a stumbling stone: Jesus. Isn't it malicious to put stones in people's way? To make Jesus the stumbling stone for Jews who have seen the goal of human life more clearly than anyone else? Or is Jesus perhaps a stumbling stone in quite a different way from that intended by Paul – not a stumbling stone for Jews but a stumbling stone for Christians? Because according to Christian faith God becomes accessible through Jesus, this Jesus becomes a stumbling stone in the dialogue with other religions, a cause of offence between Jews and Christians and indeed a scandal to us. We would very much like to grind down this stone a bit, to reduce the 'high christology', so that the Christian claim to absoluteness seems less offensive – less offensive, not only for others but for ourselves.

And now for the idea that is woven into this image. Paul formulates his complaint about Israel's unbelief with words from the message of justification: Israel has gone wrong because it has sought the righteousness of God not by faith but on the basis of works. So Jesus has become the stumbling stone. We know that the Reformation once initiated an exodus from the Middle Ages with the recognition that it is not works that make people righteous before God. That was tremendous: the break-up of a system of ecclesiastical domination which was based on the shrewd manipulation of human anxiety. And it is tion says: human dignity is independent of our actions, with which we often betray and deny this dignity. It is grounded in an unassailable Yes which is spoken to all human beings: Yes to my life, to your life, and especially to the lives of those whom neither of us like.

And now the offensive feature of this great insight: in its origin it is associated with a criticism of the law, the Torah, i.e. with what constitutes Jewish identity. There seems to be an abrupt devaluation of Jewish religion as righteousness by works at the centre of Protestant identity. What gives us pride is itself the devaluation of what for good reasons gives Jews pride. That is the dilemma with which this text confronts us if we read it as it has largely been read in Protestantism, and still is.

But did Paul want to be read like this? How did he come to write down these thoughts? He is writing in Corinth. The Corinthians had once accused him of being a poor speaker but a tremendous letter-writer Spurred on by this praise, Paul wants to write a letter on his own behalf: in a weighty letter he seeks to reject rumours that he wants to dissolve the law (the Torah), to fight Judaism and to create unrest between Jews and Gentiles. Such rumours needed to be corrected in view of his plans: Paul wanted to travel to Jerusalem, where under James the community had achieved a relatively peaceful relationship with its Jewish neighbours, and from there he wanted to go to Rome, where a dispute between Jews and Christians only a few years previously had led to the expulsion of their spokesmen. Beyond question Paul does not want to be regarded as a notorious disturber of the peace. He wants to provide a fundamental clarification of his relationship to Judaism. He wants to attest his love for it – not least so that he is welcome in Jerusalem and in Rome.

The Corinthians were probably very proud of the letter-writer Paul whom they had discovered. They probably copied out his letter several times: a copy for themselves, one for the community in Ephesus, one for the community in Rome, one for Paul – perhaps one for Jerusalem. Now I shall imagine the kind of replies Paul got.

The first reaction comes from Rabbi Gamaliel, Paul's teacher I'm giving him the words of a Jewish philosopher from the year 1990.

Among other things, Gamaliel writes to Paul: 'In your letter to the Romans I was particularly offended by the idea that Jews thought that they would be saved by actions, whereas Christians know that they will be saved solely by faith. If a Jew were to think as you imagine, then he would say to God: "Show me no gracious acts, give me no more than I deserve, but also give me no less than is my due, since I have nothing to fear." I doubt whether any Jew has ever thought like this. Every Jew knows or should know that if God were to pay him what he deserves, no more and no less, then he would be lost. His only hope hangs on the grace of God. If God decides to overlook the sorry state of his life and show him grace instead of his rights, then he has hope. But otherwise, certainly not. Paul, how could you have sketched such a caricature of Judaism as a religion of righteousness by works? I have only one answer: you were so fascinated by Jesus, so fixed on him, that nothing could compete with him, not even the Torah. So you had to criticize the Torah.

You're like someone in love with two girls one after the other. Your first love was the law. This love was true. I know that best of all. Then came your second love for God's grace in Jesus. And there you disparaged the earlier girl in order to flatter her successor all the more. That's immature. You and your followers will be reconciled with yourselves and with God, only if you recognize how precious the first love was.' Thus Gamaliel (alias Michael Wyschogrod, Professor of Philosophy in New York).

The second reaction comes from Barnabas, from whom Paul had already long parted company, though to begin with they had carried on a mission together. He writes:

'When I read your letter to the Romans I was amazed how you had developed. I know very well how your criticism of the law started. It was not criticism of the "works of the law" generally, but quite specifically of two or three things: circumcision, dietary laws and the Jewish festivals – in other

180

words only the laws which distinguish and divide Jews and Gentile in everyday life. You wanted to abolish these laws. You wanted to build up a new type of Jewish community which was open to Gentiles – in which they could become something like "honorary Jews".

Your criticism of parts of the law has meanwhile become a total criticism of the law. And it seems exaggerated. You write that the law serves only to increase sin. Do you seriously believe that the commandment to love was given to make people sin more? That's nonsense. I've only one explanation for your development: you have been attacked. There were people who wanted to re-introduce circumcision and dietary laws for Gentiles in your communities. As long as the Torah applied in principle, they could keep referring to it. So you made your criticism of the Jewish Torah more radical in order to provide no basis for such attempts. They were necessarily all invalid. By this means you wanted to defend your missionary work: your communities in which Jews and Gentiles lived together without being separated by the provisions of the law. To further the strategy of your mission you brought the law more into discredit than it really deserves. You yourself concede that it is good at the centre, and for you too the commandment to love is the summary of all the commandments. Don't you see that you can't sustain your total criticism of the law without contradiction? You're criticizing the law in this way because the church strategist in you is harnessing the theologian for his own ends. But I hope that your development is not yet at an end. Yours, Barnabas.'

James, the leader of the Jerusalem community, is the third to reply. He writes:

'Shalom! At least your letter to the Romans is a small step forward. We no longer read in it about "God's final wrath upon the Jews", as you wrote in your earliest letter, to the Thessalonians. On the contrary, now you write that all Israel will be saved. You explicitly emphasize that Israel is God's son, that God is present in it, that the covenants belong to it and that it is irrevocably loved. Nevertheless I have a few questions. They relate to apparently minor points, but your answer to them would be helpful to me in defending you against your critics in Jerusalem. You write that Israel has striven for the law of righteousness by works and not by faith. If I understand this rightly, in principle the goal is correct. The goal is the law. Only the way to it is disputed. The law is not rejected, but the view that it could be fulfilled by human action – as though one could ever realize God's will fully and completely – is. In that case Christianity would be a new way to the law – but not away from the law. Jews and Christians would still have the same goal. And when you write that Christ is the *telos* of the law, then by *telos* you would have to mean "goal" and not "end". But why didn't you make that completely clear?

You also speak of Jesus as a stumbling stone. Israel takes offence at him. But later you write that Israel has not fallen but only stumbled. It is further on the way to the goal. If I understand that rightly, then for you even those who take offence at Christ are not lost. They have only stumbled.

As I have said, it would be good if you could clear up these questions before you make an appearance here in Jerusalem. For what we have heard so far about you sometimes makes it sound as though you want to supersede and dissolve Judaism and bring the law into discredit.' Thus James.

The last to have a say is Peter, Paul's old adversary. He begins his letter with a particularly friendly form of address:

'My dear brother Paul,

We are having a vigorous debate about your letter to the Romans. I very much want to defend you against two charges: your criticism of the law and Judaism is not just a blind absolutizing of your new faith. It is not just an exaggeration for purposes of church strategy. But there is one thing that I cannot defend you against, and that is yourself. For you yourself are what you write about Judaism. That is your Judaism, before your conversion. You write that Jews are "zealots" for God who want to establish their own righteousness with good intentions, but with a false insight. You have done precisely that! You used to be a fearful zealot for the law – not out of malicious ness but with the best intentions. You once wrote that as such a zealot you surpassed all your contemporaries. Here you yourself are saying that your zeal is exceptional. Your Judaism is not representative of all Jews. But in your letter to the Romans you sometimes, though not always, depict all Jews after the pattern of your own past. Your criticism of the law hits the mark completely. I find it splendid. I agree with all of it – with one qualification: it all applies only to people like you. All this applies to people who identify themselves so fanatically with their norms and convictions that they cannot tolerate divergent minorities. You were like that. You were redeemed from this fanaticism by your conversion. And now you are projecting it on all Jews. In human terms that is certainly understandable, but nevertheless it is deeply unjust.

Don't you know that there are such fanatics everywhere? Among Christians too. You too were not always free from fanaticism as a Christian. Before your conversion you wanted to be foremost in your zeal for the law, and after your conversion you want to be foremost in criticism of the law. That's why we once fell out so sharply. So I've allowed myself to change your text in Romans at one point. That makes it run like this:

"Christians too have striven for the law of righteousness and not attained it. Why? Because they did not strive for it by faith, but through zealous works. Therefore they came up against the stone of stumbling. That lies in Zion. Only the one who builds on this stone in the midst of Israel will not be put to shame. I bear witness that Christians have a zeal for God, but it is a zeal without insight if you put pressure on minorities like the Jews who deviate from your faith. This zeal is lacking in insight into the law of God, which is summed up in the commandment to love. With such zeal and fanaticism you seek to establish your righteousness, i.e. to impose your criteria, instead of leaving it for God to decide whom he will judge righteous. You should finally recognize that Christ is the end of zeal for the law, for morality and for any conviction of faith – and that only in this way will the goal of the law, love, be fulfilled."

Dear Paul, I know that you could put this much better than I have. I am solely concerned with the simple insight that we should not look for the speck of dust in our brother's eye if we have a plank in our own eye. It would be good if you could convey that to your Gentile Christian supporters to think about – especially when they pass judgment on Jews.' Thus Peter.

And how are we to reply to Paul? I shall do so in the form of an image. Life is not merely a course, it's an examination. Especially for us, at a university, it's a permanent run-up to an examination. But everywhere, we not only go on living but constantly have to give an account of what we achieve and do. We are being tested. So life can be summed up as one great examination before the highest examining body. Of course we're afraid of failing – and the greater our knowledge of ourselves, the more we suspect that we won't pass. Paul's doctrine of justification consists of a change in the examination rules. This is the new element in Christianity, not the belief in a gracious God or a gracious examiner which we share with other religions. Normally achievements are assessed and a judgment is made at the end. But here at the start a messenger with a Galilean accent appears and tells us, 'You've passed, although you've hardly started on any of the disciplines of life.' Of course that's absurd. For some people it's a scandal. The examination is still going on; life is still being lived. But if you trust this message, then you will experience the further examination of life in a different way.

You will be able to speak more freely about things and problems. You will no longer be concerned with winning points and making an impression by what you say. You will be able openly to concede mistakes and correct them more easily. They will no longer endanger your existence and your examination.

You will be able to deal far more freely with your fellow human beings. No one will be able to set themselves up as your chief examiner any more. No one will be able to instill anxiety into you. You've already passed. But at the same time you cannot look down on those who fail in the examination.

And finally, you will become more relaxed. You will be able to concede not only that you're doing many things wrong, but also that there are wide areas of life on which you have no grip, which you hardly know. Anxiety about missing something and leaving out something is nowadays often greater than anxiety about failing.

In short, matter-of-factness, solidarity with others and relaxation in the great examination of life are the fruits of the faith which justifies. And what about those who don't believe? They will be examined by other rules. And however they behave, if you know that you would have failed before the highest examining body, then you have no reason to look down on those who toil and stumble under different examination rules. You aren't the examiner, and you should be glad that you aren't. But you know the examiner. And you know that his intentions for all are good: for my life, for your life and above all for the lives of those who are different from us.

This examiner is a stumbling stone for all of us. We shouldn't push that stumbling stone out of the way, but let it lie there: in the middle of Israel. All those who, like Paul, follow other ways because they have a different faith, may stumble over it. All may, like Paul, come through it to the faith which is the special characteristic of Christianity: now already – in the midst of life, in the midst of history – you are acquitted. Now already you are pronounced righteous. Now already you have passed. Now already you may hear God's final verdict on you. God says 'Yes' to you.

And may the peace of God which surpasses all our understanding keep your hearts and minds in Christ Jesus. Amen.

This sermon was preached in St Peter's Church, Heidelberg on 23 August 1992.

Marriage between Cornflakes and God

A marriage sermon

(Romans 15.7)

Accept each other, therefore, just as Christ has accepted you, for the glory of God.

When we hear this powerful theological statement, we do not suspect the trivial kind of problems to which it originally related. In the church in Rome there was a dispute between meat-eaters and vegetarians. To accept one another meant to accept the eating habits and cooking philosophies of others. Marriage is also about such simple things. It is often not so much the major questions which make married life difficult, but the little ones: whether one sleeps at night with the window open or shut, who gets up first in the morning, and how one squeezes toothpaste tubes most effectively. The admonition to accept each other is always appropriate in such cases. But it is no guarantee that things will go well.

Let's imagine a married couple on the morning of their silver wedding anniversary. By chance the Bible saying for their wedding day was the same as the text of this sermon. Today she puts the cornflakes on the table in a particularly loving way. For since their first breakfast together after the wedding he has kept saying, 'How good to begin the day with cornflakes.' But today, on the twenty-fifth anniversary of their wedding, he bangs the table and shouts, 'At least you could have spared me your cornflakes today!' She is absolutely flabbergasted. 'But that's your favourite food in the morning,' she says. However, he firmly replies: 'Today is the hour of truth. Haven't you ever noticed that I hate cornflakes? But when you put them in front of me on the day after our wedding I still had our pastor's unfortunate sermon ringing in my ears. "Accept one another," he had said, and explained that this originally referred to eating habits. Other people's eating habits have to be accepted. We all have our own philosophies here. I thought that you had a cornflakes philosophy, and I wanted to accept it – purely out of love for you. And the more it cost me to eat cornflakes, the greater my love for you seemed to me to be.' For her, too, the wedding day becomes the hour of truth. For she confesses that for a long time now she would really have much preferred rolls to cornflakes, but for love of him she had refrained from making the change.

Dear people, here we have a moderate sermon catastrophe of the kind that I certainly want to avoid. So I shall say to you, 'Accept each other – but please, not like that!' Accept each other by clearly indicating your likes and dislikes. Don't expect your partner to have the gift of telepathy.

That brings me to the second part of the text. Paul doesn't only write 'Accept each other'; he adds 'for the glory of God'. Even those who find it difficult to talk of God as easily as people talk of God in church can perhaps get a sense that belief in God includes the insight that we are not God but human beings, imperfect human beings. And that is important for any relationship and partnership.

God discovers what we want before we have expressed our wishes. But human couples and partners have to communicate their wishes; otherwise there is the cornflakes effect. God surrounds us everywhere. God supports us unconditionally and has made an irrevocable covenant with each of us. But there are limitations to the nearness of human beings; they can give us only limited support, provide only limited help. They cannot have unlimited burdens imposed on them. We are not to expect anyone to take God's place for us in our relationships. Our partners are always imperfect human beings. But above all, we ourselves are imperfect. None of those who have had a happy marriage will say in retrospect that they were ready for marriage when they entered into it. Nor will they say that they've learned everything about it. Those who get married and lead a married life will always be imperfect and unprepared. Before we got married, my wife and I saw a film which was called 'the Perfect Marriage'. We saw a perfect couple. They were both attractive, both young, both dynamic, both successful, both healthy. But at that time we promised each other that we would not have a perfect marriage. That was a remarkable promise to make at the beginning of a marriage, but it's helped us a great deal.

'Accept each other for the glory of God.' That means: accept each other as imperfect human beings, as those who know that God alone is perfect. But of course this imperfection is also a problem: how does one cope with one's lifelong imperfection – in marriage?

That brings me to the third part of the text. Paul doesn't just say, 'Accept each other,' but, 'Accept each other, therefore, just as Christ has accepted you, for the glory of God.' Christ accepted imperfect people. This statement is the most important thing that I can say to you all today. I've spent a long time thinking how to put it in such a way that it reaches your heart, penetrates to that point where you are quite alone with yourselves and with God, to the place where the decisions of life are made. Again I must ask you to give rein to your imagination a little.

Just imagine that we are gathered in the presence of God before the creation of the world. Fortunes on earth are being distributed. Each person is given a role. I, too, am offered various kinds of life. To the first offer I say, 'No, please, not this narrow life. I want to get to know the whole world. I don't want to be shut up in such a small country, however attractive it may be.'

To the second offer I say, 'No, please, not this life. Give me a handsome and healthy body. The thought of being weaker than others all my life gets me down.'

And I turn down even the third offer: 'No, please, not this life with people who are often sad. I can't bear it when other people sink into themselves, unsettle me by their silence and break off contact.'

I even reject a further offer: 'Please, not this life with a constant fear of failure. I want to be more successful than the rest.'

Of course, I'm getting worried that I'm trying the patience of the Most High too much. But he is incomprehensibly kind. He says, 'If you aren't content with any of these roles, then I want to show you the role I have chosen for myself. Perhaps that will help you to choose your own life.'

And God says, 'I shall live in a small land. My longest journey will be no more than sixty miles from my birthplace. I shall have no house or steady occupation. I shall give up my original occupation. Although I shall show signs of being very gifted at the age of twelve, I shall not be an academic, but rather develop a great antipathy to scholars. I shall have a few friends, but they will forsake me at the decisive moment. I shall not grow old, but die a miserable death, the victim of a whim of the state.'

I say to God, 'Lord, how will you achieve anything great on earth in this miserable role? Is that how you plan to make the creation achieve your goal for it?'

And he replies, 'I shall convince people that I love them because I am near to them. I shall change them more by love than by power and force. And if you too love your life, you will change more that way than by all the force that you might apply.'

I concede that it is verging on obstinacy when I now say, 'Lord, in your sovereign freedom and love it's easy for you to accept such a miserable life. But I'm an imperfect human being, a poor worm. I'm not so free, I'm not so sovereign.'

And God says, 'Believe, only believe me – and you will have a share in this freedom and sovereignty.'

I spontaneously ask, 'then at least give me a large portion of this faith.'

But he shakes his head: 'You will get only the normal endowment – and also a normal portion of doubt. And if by chance you should be born in Swabia, don't believe the rumour that people in this land are more pious from birth onwards than they are elsewhere.

But as you're so faint-hearted, I have some more help for you. I've arranged the creation in such a way that people value and love one another – in friendship and sympathy, in shared work and shared leisure time. And for you and many others I've provided something special.

There is someone in the world who will love you more than anything else. You will find that person. And that person will find you. I shall accept your mutual choice and bless your relationship.

You will share everything: table and bed, body and thoughts, home and money, rolls and cornflakes, memories and plans, success and failure, happiness and sorrow.

If you find it difficult to accept your life – it is accepted by that person's love. That person will help you to say yes to yourself. And if that person finds it difficult to accept this – your love will help.

You may both be the image of my love for my creatures through your mutual love. You are both my children.

And I will give you two gifts which will help you a great deal, hope and humour – humour so that you can laugh at yourselves, at your little cornflakes catastrophes and your lifelong imperfections.

Dear people,

May God give you all this in your hearts: faith, love, hope and a touch of humour. Today it may be easier than at other times to feel that life is good and beautiful. But I know that on days like this some people feel their loneliness and disappointment even more deeply. None of us is spared dark hours – and sometimes years, tormentingly long years. So I would like to say to all of you, 'Accept each other, as Christ has accepted you.' In him God has shown that he does not want to be with imaginary or perfect people but with people who really exist, with people like you and me, with people like this couple.

When they say Yes to each other, then say this Yes softly with them – as a Yes to their relationship, as a Yes to your life, as a Yes to your fellow men and women. And even if you don't feel it now, your Yes is an answer to a great Yes that God has always already said to your life and will say to all eternity. We often fail to hear it. We get caught up in our suffering, in our failure, our frustration and our aggressions. But God keeps wanting to penetrate our hardness with this Yes and to assure each of us, 'You are loved. You are a precious and valuable person. You are the image of God, you are a thought of God.' I hope that both of you hear the many voices saying this Yes, all the love and friendship that so many people are offering you. And that when you look back on your wedding you will be able to say, 'that was a good saying that we chose.'

Accept each other, therefore, just as Christ has accepted you, for the glory of God.

And last but not least, I hope that it will not take you until your silver wedding anniversary to discover what you really prefer, rolls or cornflakes.

And may the peace of God which surpasses all our understanding keep our hearts and minds in Christ Jesus. Amen.

This sermon was given on 1 September 1990. The cornflakes story came to me through oral tradition.

The Sympathetic Sides of the Catholic Understanding of Marriage

A sermon at an ecumenical wedding

(Romans 15.7)

Accept each other, just as Christ has accepted us

Paul's invitation is addressed to two conflicting groups in the Roman church: a group which in principle ate no meat, and another which made eating meat almost a confessional question. This was a kind of confessional dispute. So this text is an excellent one for a marriage which brings together two confessions.

The somewhat portentous phrase 'brings together two confessions' expresses a hope, namely that marriages like this will become the forerunners of a wider and deeper bond between the churches. Individual Christians have greater freedoms to come closer to one another than bishops and synods. They can undermine barriers which still exist between the confessions. We could say that many Catholic-Protestant marriages succeed better than the churches in accepting each other as Christ has accepted them. So my first wish for you is that you should live out your marriage in such a way that at least in this respect bishops and synods can take you as an example.

But the opposite is also the case: the relationship between the Catholic and the Protestant churches can be a model for a marriage, especially in the later years of marriages. Beyond question, there is friction between the churches on many points. A true Protestant like me will always have difficulties with the three Ps: the Pope, the Priesthood and the Pill. And nowadays the difficulties are even increasing, say, because the Protestant churches are making women pastors, while women are in principle excluded from the Catholic priesthood. And conversely, when even progressive Catholic theologians are asked whether the Protestant churches are true churches, one will hear the reply, 'In principle, yes, but ...'

So we should have no illusions about the barriers and problems which continue to exist. No sooner have we solved a few problems than new ones crop up. So we should be delighted that we have found ways of living together well, with imagination and patience, wisdom and humour – that churches visit one another, that pastors are friendly with priests, that today it is quite natural for us to be able to celebrate this wedding together. We have learned to see what we have in common and also to experience what is alien as enrichment. So we have learned to accept one another, despite some sore points.

Precisely for that reason the relationship between the confessions can be the model for a wedding. Every couple discovers sooner or later the sore points caused by friction. These may begin with little things, like the temperature at which the central hearing should be set – and end with strategies for dealing with mother-in-law.

So my second wish for you is that with imagination and patience, wisdom and humour you should keep finding ways of keeping together – even if some questions remain unresolved. Measure the success of your marriage not by whether there are problems or not, but by how you deal with these problems and how you overcome them. In my view the decisive thing is not just to forgive the other laboriously for being different, but also to learn to love the differences. That is as true for ecumenical relations as it is for marriage. I want to speak quite personally and give you an example to make this clear. I have a secret sympathy for the Catholic understanding of marriage – despite all the differences connected with the three Ps mentioned above. I have discovered something in the Catholic understanding of marriage which has attracted me a great deal – and I want to pass it on to you and the whole congregation.

According to the Catholic understanding, marriage is a sacrament; something by which God communicates salvation to his creatures and helps them towards a fulfilled and successful life – now and in eternity. Here is a place where God is near to people. By contrast, Protestants think that God is near anywhere in the world – as much in one's job as at home, as much in washing and cooking as in the office and factory. 'Marriage is a worldly thing,' said Luther, and by that he meant that God is as near and as away in it as anywhere in our life.

Here in principle I'm thinking in an utterly Protestant way, but I've made three discoveries from our Catholic friends.

The first discovery is that God is indeed present everywhere. So one cannot mark out any place in life as particularly 'holy'. But God does not allow himself to be found everywhere in the same way. We find this more where two people act together in love than where they fall out in disputes. We find it where two partners in a marriage say Yes unreservedly to each other, in such a way that one feels that this Yes is an echo of the great Yes that God said to his creation when he said, 'And behold, it was all very good.' We find it where two partners in a marriage accept each other though one is sick, going through a crisis, unhappy. We find it where 'accept each other as Christ has accepted you' is lived out and not just preached. For Christ has not accepted imaginary people, but real people, people like you and me, people like this couple. If everything by means of which God helps life to be fulfilled and his presence to be experienced is a sacrament, then I can immediately understand why marriage can be regarded as a sacrament, as something which is holy and communicates salvation. So my wish for you is that you should also experience your love as something holy – as something that is sheltered in a greater love that embraces us in our mother's womb and still embraces us in death.

And now my second discovery. In the Catholic understanding, the sacrament of marriage also includes sexual union as an expression of mutual affection. This affection is an end in itself. No one may make it a means for other ends. No one may instrumentalize it for the purpose of enjoyment or career or having children. Love and affection are an end in themselves. That is the only way in which we can create a space for our children in which they too feel accepted for their own sakes. It is most successful when the parents also accept each other – for their own sakes, as they are, body and soul, with their whole body, with tender gestures and actions. For that is the language which children also understand at a very early age. And it's a language which we still understand into old age, when other means of communication fail to reach us: the language of the body. So my wish for you is that you should experience your love as something that embraces the whole body – not only now when you are young, but all through your lives. 'Accept one another, as Christ has accepted you' also means 'Let your bodies become the language of love.' Become one flesh, as the Bible says. For God, too, became flesh in Christ and in this way showed his creatures his love.

Now to my third discovery. Protestants often criticize the division between priests and laity in Catholicism. But few know that this division is partly done away with in marriage. The partners in a marriage give each other the sacrament of marriage. They take the role of the priest. They practise something of the priesthood of all believers. When they promise each other love and faithfulness at the altar, the priest is only their assistant, no more. Furthermore, when the couple give each other the sacrament of marriage, they are acting with equal rights. Here there is no distinction between man and woman. All the distinctions that we have difficulty overcoming in our actual marriages fall away – not least in the correction of Christian ideas which are centuries old. Precisely for that reason it should be emphasized that the view of marriage as a sacrament sets both partners side by side, with equal rights, and make each the subject of the action towards the other. So my wish for you is that you should experience yourselves in your marriage as equal partners – especially if it should prove that there are inequalities here, that one is in some respects weaker than the other, less skilled or less successful. Particularly in that case there is proof of this fundamental equality of the rights of the partners before God, which is independent of your fortunes and your capacities, and which no one may shake.

Perhaps you can now understand why I have some sympathy for the Catholic understanding of marriage. Here I have found a tremendous affirmation of life, which is warm-hearted and human, namely that there is something sacred about a marriage, that it is based on body-language and on the equality of the partners. All these three features are closely connected with the understanding of marriage as a sacrament. Protestants may not share this view, but they can share what is expressed in it. Here we can learn from one another.

For that is what I hope for you above all: that you should learn from one another. Don't just excuse the other for being different, but attempt to love this other and experience the otherness as an enrichment. That is true of ecumenical relations. It is true of marriage. It is even more true of an ecumenical marriage. You have a special opportunity here. You will grasp it if you follow the text for your marriage,

Accept each other, just as Christ has accepted us.

If you do this, the peace of God will fill your hearts and your home and you will bring some light into a world which is often very dark and cold. Amen.

This wedding sermon was given on 8 September 1990. My interpretation of the Catholic understanding of marriage follows the more humane variants of the Catholic doctrine of marriage. I am aware that the close connection between sacrament and sexuality can also primarily be grounded in the purpose of having children. But in the light of the biblical foundation of the Catholic understanding of marriage (Eph.5.22-23, where the Vulgate translates 'mystery' in 5.32 as *sacramentum*), the orientation of the sexual union on the communion of love between husband and wife keeps breaking through. Nowhere in Eph.5.22-33 is there mention of having children. I need not emphasize differences in the Protestant and Catholic understandings of marriage, e.g. the different attitudes to divorce.

Everyday Conflicts and God's Longing for the Human Being

(James 4.1–10)

Those conflicts and disputes among you, where do they come from? Do they not come from your cravings that are at war within you? You want something and do not have it; so you commit murder. And you covet something and cannot obtain it; so you engage in disputes and conflicts. You do not have, because you do not ask. You ask and do not receive, because you ask wrongly, in order to spend what you get on your pleasures. Adulterers! Do you not know that friendship with the world is enmity with God? Therefore whoever wishes to be a friend of the world becomes an enemy of God. Or do you suppose that it is for nothing that the scripture says, 'God yearns jealously for the spirit that he has made to dwell in us'? But he gives all the more grace; therefore it says, 'God opposes the proud, but gives grace to the humble.'

Submit yourselves therefore to God. Resist the devil, and he will flee from you. Draw near to God, and he will draw near to you. Cleanse your hands, you sinners, and purify your hearts, you double-minded. Lament and mourn and weep. Let your laughter be turned into mourning and your joy into dejection. Humble yourselves before the Lord, and he will exalt you.

Where do the conflicts among you come from? And the disputes? That's the question that the text puts to us. It doesn't ask, 'Why is there so much conflict in the world?' It asks about the conflict in the community, among us. It is not looking for a theoretical answer, but a practical answer. It is seeking to help us to see our conflicts in a new light and to cope with them in a different way.

198

What is strange in this question is the extension of it to murder and killing. We suddenly hear the charge, 'You commit murder.' That seems so out of keeping with the skirmishes in the community that there are those who think that here a copyist changed a couple of letters. Here the Greek 'envy' became 'murder', *phthoneite* became *phoneuete*. Be this as it may, unfortunately the development from envy to murder takes place not only on paper and papyrus but often enough also in reality. The wickedness which is resorted to in the conflicts of everyday life needs only to be co-ordinated, to be directed against a goal or a group of people – and already everyday prejudice becomes murder and killing. We experience it almost every week – in our own country.

So the question 'Where do these conflicts among you come from?' is a legitimate one. The answer given in the Letter of James causes difficulties. It reduces the problem to one great 'either-or', which it hammers home to its hearers and readers in three variants.

The first 'either-or' sounds very theological: God or the world – that's the alternative.

The second 'either-or' sounds mythological: God or the devil – that's the question here. 'submit yourselves to God and resist the devil' is what we read.

The third 'either-or' sounds psychological, but nevertheless somewhat old-fashioned: God or the passions. Or more precisely, humility or passion. The cause of conflicts between people is ultimately the conflict of passions within them.

The Letter of James wants us to make a decision against the world, against the devil, against the passions. Here these three dark entities fuse together. It also says that this decision calls for mourning, for separation from much that is valuable to us. Good-bye to laughter and joy in the world. And what does it promise instead? It promises nearness to God. Draw near to God and God will draw near to you. Humble yourselves and God will exalt you – i.e. bring you near to him.

That's my short version of the text. And now my question to you is: Isn't that very sectarian? The wicked world there and the community here? Satan there and God here? The passions there and humility here? Isn't everything in black and white?

Furthermore, isn't this text hostile to life? Friendship with God at the expense of laughter and joy in the world?

Probably Christianity today lives by quite a different text. In the modern world belief in God means friendship with the world, at least a friendly relationship with creation. Belief in God means the end of polluting creation. Belief in God at least means a great passion – the passion to live and not have your life lived for you. But at first the text of the Letter of James sounds quite different.

Because I love the Letter of James, I want to bring you closer to this text, too. So I shall tell you how Little James became a friend of the world – in the sense that 'friendship with the world' is understood in the Letter of Big James.

Little James had to learn the meaning of 'You want something and do not have it. And you covet something and cannot obtain it.' He learned it when his little sister was born. Then he was envious of the baby which was receiving so much care and attention through breast-feeding, bathing, changing and cuddling – whereas he suddenly had to be content with very much less. At that time he discovered a successful strategy for still getting attention. His slogan was, 'When I can't get anything I begin to whine.' That's the way it is in the world: the person who complains most gets something in the end.

Kindergarten brought further progress. Here Little James didn't get anywhere in the fight for toys by whining. A direct punch, aimed at Susie's chest, was more successful. Susie ran crying to the teacher. And Little James got a lecture on the theme, 'You must not hit.' Next time there was a quarrel over toys, Susie got her revenge with a powerful kick. Now he ran crying to the teacher and complained. 'susie hit me!' And he was told, 'But James, why didn't you defend yourself?' So he learned the strategy of pulling his punches so that they weren't hard enough to make Susie cry, and so that the teacher wasn't called in. In this way, to use our academic terms, he had internalized one of the most important basic rules in the skill of getting on in society, namely, 'Administer in small doses to others what you would not want them to do to you.'

James was to take yet a third step towards becoming a friend of the world. In the long run Susie stopped being influenced by small punches. So Little James began to negotiate, 'Please give me that train and I'll give you two pieces of chewing gum.' And he whispered in her ear, 'Yesterday Mary let me have the train for one piece. But because you're you and we get on so well together I'll give you two pieces. But that must be our secret.' Of course he'd invented the business with Mary. And so he learned the third basic rule of this world: 'What cannot be had by naughtiness can be got better by diplomacy.'

We were all socialized like Little James. As well as the official curriculum of respect and fairness we learned the unofficial curriculum of crying, measured naughtiness and diplomatic trips. And so we became what the Letter of James calls 'friends of the world'. Friends of a world of whining, in which the one who whines most gets most. Friends of a world of measured naughtiness: the one who places his punches skilfully within the rules wins. Friends of a world of diplomacy which gets at the other by means of the ear.

Little James grew bigger. He learned that not only the kindergarten but the whole world is a dispute over opportunities in life. Not just over toys, but over everything: food and clothing, possessions and status. One of his teachers at school passed on a comforting thought. This world of disputes isn't everything. A piece of bread gets smaller and smaller, the more one has to divide it. But a piece of knowledge gets bigger and bigger, the more one disseminates it. The fight over the distribution of opportunities in life stops in the world of the intellect, art and science.

So James went to the university – the gateway to the world of the mind – with great expectations. He heard a lecture on ethics. But instead of passing on his own insights, the lecturer engaged in vigorous criticism of others – especially attacking the errors of a so-called 'Cultman school'. Every time he mentioned a book from this school he moved from the desk to the waste-paper basket and made a gesture of tearing it up – and the book to which he was referring landed, with all its errors, in the waste-paper basket. Here, too, the rule seemed to apply: 'Do in a measured (and sometimes malicious) way to others what you would not want them to do to you.'

James now knew that, with small differences, the same rules applied in the world of the intellect as they did in the kindergarten. Therefore he continued his quest for a world beyond the everyday conflicts and struggles over distribution. Here he happened to wander into a university service. By chance the sermon was about James 4.

The preacher had just explained the three great 'either-ors' in the Letter of James. He began as modern preachers tend to do, with psychology – with the alternative of humility or passion. He made excuses for using the old-fashioned word 'humility', saying that it meant something like voluntarily occupying a lowly position. And then he remarked:

'It all depends to whom this is being said. Is it being said to those in a quite lowly position, or to those who are in a high position?' In James it is clear who is being addressed: he has just been speaking of teachers who take pride in their wisdom, and then of rich merchants who plan profitable business, but forget that all their plans can go up in smoke. But to the little and the lowly the Letter of James says, 'Let the one who is lowly boast in being raised up' (1.9). For in James' community the commandment to love is the ruling factor. That calls for equal treatment of all, without respect for persons. Those who are lowly and bowed down are to be raised up in the community. They are to gain self-respect. And those who are great and rich and learned are to practise humility.

So isn't the text addressed to all of us? By no means. Certainly we don't want to be rich, but we do want to be a bit better off than others. We know that learning isn't everything, but at least we want to be a bit more learned than the rest. So aren't we always getting in one another's way? The text tells all of us, 'If you give up some of your goals, you will become freer in the everyday war.'

At least it's clear that those who are convinced that money isn't everything can cope more easily with the loss of money. Those who think that reports aren't everything can cope better with bad reports. And of course it's easier to give up the dream of a colourful and brilliant artistic life if one arrives at the insight that even grey mice can live well.

I know that all this isn't a problem for many of us. So I must also add that sometimes it's also important to bid farewell to the longing for harmony. This longing is particularly widespread among Christians. But it often sharpens conflicts. It exposes the partner in a conflict to the moral charge of being a great disrupter.

We all find it difficult to say farewell to these and many other longings and wishes. That is why the Letter of James is right when it calls for mourning: 'Let your laughter be turned into mourning and your joy into dejection.

Note that this is said to those who laugh, to those who live in joy, to those who are above everyday wrangles. But what are we to say to those who feel helpless? To those who are sad? To those who are the bottom of the pile?

Here I want to bring I in the second 'either-or', God or the devil. Of course we must demythologize the devil. The devil is the world, experienced as a seductive temptation and conflict – either as enjoyment in being entangled with it or as a temptation to give up in resignation. If we resist this temptation, then the devil departs from us. If we draw near to God, then God draws near to us. That means that we aren't a battlefield between two alien powers. We aren't helplessly given over to them. The decision is for us to make. The devil becomes the devil only if we are subject to him. It is our faith that makes God God.

Transferring this mythology into the everyday world, I would want to answer the question 'When does the devil have you in his grasp?' like this. The devil has you in his grasp when you're lying in bed in the morning and telling yourself that everything is unutterably wretched. You say to yourself, 'I'm ignored and pushed around. I'm worthless. I can't get anywhere.' But you can. You can, once you've contradicted this voice. Contradict this voice and it will stop nagging at you from within. Stop Satan's mouth – and he will shut up. Luther recommended a powerful fart in such situations. But of course this Lutheran fart therapy is not a panacea.

Rather, the third 'either-or' is the decisive one: God or the world. This 'either-or' applies to everyone: both to those who are up at the top and those who are right down at the bottom. The Letter of James is not so naive as to think that belief in God is itself a standpoint beyond conflict. Certainly it says, 'You dispute and are at war and have nothing because you do not pray (to God).' But just praying, or asking, as this translation has it, does not achieve anything by itself. For the letter continues, 'You ask and do not receive, because you ask wrongly, in order to spend what you get on your pleasures.' The Letter of James already knows that one can misuse faith and religion to get on better in the fight over the distribution of opportunities and commodities in the world. One can praise prayer for making people fit in the everyday war. One can seek spirituality – with meditation exercises and deep mental soundings – to harden oneself inwardly for the everyday life of the world.

To those who get caught up in this everyday war – with or without religious trimmings – James exclaims, 'You adulterers! You're violating the spirit of God which dwells in you.' What he means is not the Holy Spirit, but the spirit that God breathed into Adam, the spirit that makes the human being the image of God. Here the letter of James quotes an unknown scriptural text: 'God yearns jealously for the spirit that he has made to dwell in us', God jealously strives after his image. He is full of anxiety because his image can be damaged in the world. Because it risks getting lost if you hurl yourself into the everyday war over power, possessions and education. God is jealous. Because he wants us to behave as his image – and not as the images of apes. These wrangles over food and hierarchy – sometimes with direct force, sometimes with diplomacy. And they keep on and on doing it with enjoyment. But you are people who in all your conflicts at the same time should also rise above them – just a God rises above them when he makes his sun shine on good and evil, just and unjust, friends and enemies, apes great and small. You are the image of this God.

This God is no God without passions. God longs for you because you are too good to fall under the wheel of the world's wars, great and small. God is sharp towards you. God has invested a great deal in you. Precisely for that reason God can help you to control your passions – your goals, wishes and desires. Only then will you really become one with God. Only then will you be undivided. For that is the great image that runs through the Letter of James: the image of someone who does not have 'two souls', someone whose life is not split.

For where do the conflicts and disputes among you come from? In the end they arise because you live in conflict with yourself – because your greed, your desires, your competitive feelings alienate you from yourself.

It might seem that I've lost sight of our James. But that's not the case.

Perhaps you too are a James (or a Jemima). Perhaps you've already won in everyday life – with a successful mixture of whining, small wickednesses and diplomacy. If you have, don't be proud. No one is spared having to bid farewell to their dreams and wishes.

But perhaps you've already been dealt a severe blow in the everyday war of the world. And you're still full of resentment. That's not a bad thing. No one can ride over the petty everyday wars in a sovereign way.

But you should know that the power of God, God's life-force dwells in you. This power helps you to live in the wrangles and pressures of the world – instead of having your life controlled by the world and its wrangles. But you should both know that

205

God longs for you. God longs for both of you. He longs for the spirit which he has made to dwell in you.

And may the peace of God that surpasses all our reason keep our hearts and minds in Jesus Christ. Amen.

A sermon given in St Peter's Church, Heidelberg on 4 July 1993 – at the end of a semester during which I endured some highly unpleasant 'everyday conflicts'. .

Music – A Parable of God

A sermon at a music service

(I Corinthians 4.1-5)

Think of us in this way, as servants of Christ and stewards of God's mysteries. Moreover, it is required of stewards that they be found trustworthy. But with me it is a very small thing that I should be judged by you or by any human court. I do not even judge myself. I am not aware of anything against myself, but I am not thereby acquitted. It is the Lord who judges me. Therefore do not pronounce judgment before the time, before the Lord comes, who will bring to light the things now hidden in darkness and will disclose the purposes of the heart. Then each one will receive commendation from God.

Vivaldi: The great Gloria

Paul's situation as presented in the text for this sermon is familiar to us. Paul is standing before the tribunal of his community. He understands himself as a steward of the mysteries of God. But his opponents say that his motives are impure. What is manifested in his preaching is not God, but something that is human, all too human. The accused concedes, 'I'm certainly unaware of any impure motives, but that doesn't mean that I'm right. For I can't see through myself. I can't see what is going on in my unconscious. Only God can see that. And only before God's tribunal will the hidden things of the heart be made manifest.'

In the modern world we are always standing before a tribunal, the tribunal of reason. We have to justify everything to it: our experiences, our actions, our habits, our feelings and our faith. The whole of life is tribunalized, and an explanation is required of everyone. Of religion above all, which, like Paul in his time, has fallen into disrepute today: the accusation is that behind the mysteries of God there is something that is human, all-too-human, something of which we are unconscious. It is our product, which we disguise as a divine mystery.

Today everything has to justify itself before this tribunal, even those things that are apparently unproblematical, even beauty, even music. So far music has had an easier time than religion defending itself, though it too is difficult to justify. What use is it? What truth does it convey? What does it prove? Before the tribunal of reason it has to answer this question – that is, unless it takes the only successful defensive strategy and firmly says that there must be something in life that does not need to justify itself, something that is not just useful, and precisely for that reason is a parable which frees us from all compulsions to offer any justification.

When I was studying theology, in long discussions we cross-examined faith before the tribunal of our reason. I recall discussions about God. They focussed on the question whether God is a person who discloses himself only through his word or a kind of systemic property of the universe, or even an invention of our imagination. At that time I shocked one of my old teachers with the thesis that God is like music: from the outside apparently a systemic property of waves and frequencies, but if we open ourselves to it wholly and completely, a powerful voice which addresses us and seizes us, we know not how. At that time my teacher raised his hands in horror. One couldn't say anything like that. God as music? No, for God's sake, no! I hope my old teacher will forgive me as today I disseminate such heresies from the pulpit and do so in the framework of a music service – though I'm certain that Vivaldi's Gloria will by now have softened even the hardest orthodox hearts present.

So I shall stand by the thesis of my youth, though now in keeping with my more mature years I shall put it more carefully: music is not a parable of God, but it can become a parable of God. If I had to defend belief in God before the tribunal of reason, at all events I would want to have music as a witness. My plea would run like this.

So you think that only human experience lies behind the mysteries of God. But listen to this music. Beyond question it has been devised by human beings and played by human beings. An infinite amount of laborious work is involved in each successful performance. But if it is successful, the traces of that laborious work are blotted out. The disciplining of the fingers, the hands, the breath – the aim of all this is to dispel the memory of the disciplining. Although beyond question music is composed, produced and played by us, we experience it in its successful forms as a kind of 'revelation'. It opens up a world of its own. And as in the case of religion, we puzzle over the question 'Who has revealed it?' Does it come from the unconscious depths of our heart? Or the depths of reality – an objective power which grasps us before we understand it?

There is no doubt that both religion and music are made by human beings. But if we enter into them, we experience an encounter with an enigmatic reality which we have not made. Here this reality is not the same in religion as it is in music. But there is at least a formal affinity. And because of this affinity, any music can become a parable of God, especially music in worship. Its special characteristic is that not only can it become such a parable for God, but it *seeks* to become such a parable – a parable for God's promise and claim, for God's comfort and God's demands. I want to demonstrate both these things.

As for comfort, let me say something about my experience with music. There is a piece by Johannes Brahms which I keep listening to when bitterness and hurt threaten to poison life emotionally – whether among other people whom I meet or in myself. It begins with a forlorn alto voice lamenting in gloomy and sorry tones that some things have got lost in life. The words are by Goethe, who wrote them after meeting a deeply unhappy person:

But who is that, on one side?
His track loses itself in the bushes;
behind him spring back the twigs together;
the grass stands up again:
the desert swallows him up.

Ah, who will heal the sorrows
of him for whom balsam turned to poison?
Who drank hatred of men
from the abundance of love!
Once disdained, now a disdainer,
he feeds secretly on his own worth
in unsatisfying selfishness.

There are also people among us today who are struggling with this problem, marvellous and precious people who will not see their own value, people who risk getting lost because they have been so deeply hurt. They have experienced so much as scorn – and are now scornful themselves. If you tell them, 'You did really well,' they take you to imply that they usually do things badly. If you whisper to them how young they look, they think that at other times they look old and haggard. Such an unfortunate person, in danger of getting lost in life, crouches in all of us.

Then, after the long solitary alto lament in this Brahms rhapsody, the choir begins in a bright C major and accompanies the solo voice with the following prayer:

If there is on your psaltery,
O father of Love, one sound
acceptable to his ear,
refresh his heart with it!
Open his overclouded gaze
to the thousand springs
close by him who thirsts
in the desert.

The alto voice joins in this chorale. Sometimes it detaches itself from the choir and mixes its sorrow with their confidence. But it is no longer alone. It is interwoven with the many voices of the choir.

What this example conveys is true of all music in worship. All our music, all our singing, is intercession for others, is intercession also for you, even without words or intent. We are singing and making music here to assure you that you are not alone with your suffering. And you should know that no one is without suffering. If we examine our lives honestly before the tribunal of our reason, each one of us has to acknowledge that there is a painful contradiction between what we wanted and what we have done. There is a contradiction between our longing for happiness and the disappointments of life. But precisely for that reason we are now asking you nevertheless to join in the praise of God. At least let your lament be accompanied by our praise. Here you are not standing before the tribunal of reason which measures your life by strict criteria. Nor are you standing before a tribunal of people who are all too aware of the things you have done wrong and badly. You are in a community which is proclaiming the praise of God and singing the Gloria. For God is the only authority who finally and for ever says Yes to your life, the only authority which can free us from all pressure to justify ourselves. God is an authority which I nowhere feel more clearly than where I unconditionally affirm life, although I cannot justify it.

Thus music can become a parable of God's promise – but at the same time it is a parable of God's claim, God's demand on us.

Perhaps you've come to this music service simply to listen to the music and not the sermon. That's an honourable motive. You're welcome. Nevertheless, I've something else to say to you. You shouldn't just enjoy music; you should make music. There is no service at which people aren't asked to join in the singing. You can't say, 'But I'm unmusical.' That doesn't matter. For nothing gives singing in the church its unmistakable colouring and beauty so much as the many wrong notes. And if you hear someone singing wrong notes loudly, you're all the more aware that they come from the heart. The organ can cope with everything, including your wrong notes.

That's how it is throughout life. God is like powerful music. But it's a music which we can't hear without getting involved. The theme is there. You haven't chosen your fellow musicians. The music has begun. But it hasn't yet finished. It is missing a note. It is missing the note of your voice. Nor will your voice be the last. Because it is so difficult to put experiences with music (especially God's music) into words, I want to quote another poem. It's a nature poem by Wilhelm Lehmann.

> The winter lime, the summer lime
> bloom separately –
> in between, dear son,
> the song comes to an end
>
> ...
> Rain spots the grey stones,
> the yellow hammer needs
> the last note of its song,
> sing it, my son.

If like this poem you understand the whole of creation as God's hidden music, you will know that the last note is always missing. You have to add it yourself. But you, too, do not bring it to an end. Sometimes our sons continue more convincingly what we have begun.

At the moment one of my sons is in South Africa. He wanted to do social work in a black township in Johannesburg. He entered a world in which new hopes have been raised – but in which violence is constantly increasing. He experienced murders and death threats which prevented him from doing as much work as he had planned. But he also met a priest who despite the death threats made against him goes into such a township every day to fight against hatred, violence and hopelessness.

Is that also part of God's great music? Yes it is. We share the responsibility for how it goes on. We share the responsibility for the shrill tones of the hatred and the distorted voices of violence in South Africa in Yugoslavia, in the Near East, and at home.

But – someone might say – does that fit into the great Gloria? Yes it does. For in the middle of this Gloria we hear the words, 'We give you thanks, Jesus Christ, who bears the sins of the world, have mercy upon us.' At the heart of the great music of this world, at its centre, stands the shrill dissonance of the cross. And from this point onwards, at least, anyone listening to this music cannot continue to enjoy it as much as before, out of an awareness of being inextricably bound up with those who today are collapsing under the sins of the world. Such a person is aware of being irrevocably bound up with the one who collapsed under the sins of the world – in order to overcome them. It is our task to continue his theme in many variations.

Will this enable us to stand before the tribunal of our reason? Will this acquit us before God's tribunal – that tribunal the outlines of which can still be recognized behind the court of our reason? The text of this sermon, which speaks of this tribunal of God, ends in a surprising way. The judge does not condemn anyone. He gives praises to them all.

That is not our business. Our business is to sing the praise of God. But if God allows music in his tribunal and accepts our praise, then everything has already changed. A courtroom full of music is no longer a courtroom. It has become a concert hall, in which no one has been condemned. If we no longer experience reality under the image of a gigantic tribunal, but as great music – music which includes the shrillest dissonances, music which changes us from listeners to players, music which does not exclude anyone from joining in – then we have a share in God's reality. We are ourselves part of this reality, which does not need to be justified, and cannot be justified, because it alone has the power to justify everything and bring even the most incomplete music of our life to a good ending.

Then the beginning of the Gloria will become reality. *Gloria in excelsis Deo et in terra pax hominibus bonae voluntatis.* Glory to God in the highest and on earth peace to men of good will.

May this peace of God which surpasses all our understanding, keep your hearts and minds in Christ Jesus, Amen.

This sermon was given in St Peter's Church, Heidelberg on 15 December 1991. Vivaldi's great Gloria was performed before and after the sermon.

Art as Sign Language of Faith

Theological meditations on the Heidelberg window designs of Johannes Schreiter

Every now and then Heidelberg University has open days. All its institutes are open and attempt to give a presentation of their work that anyone can understand. Some find it easy. The natural sciences have marvellous equipment with which one can not only do research but play. Another institute can display a copy of our Chancellor's dissertation. But we theologians are always in difficulty. I have sat on committees racking their brains about how to demonstrate visibly and attractively in a short space of time what theology, and above all theology today, is: an exciting existential and intellectual adventure, concerned with the timeless questions of human life. Recently, however, it occurred to me what we could show: the Heidelberg window designs of Johannes Schreiter. Through them, I think, one can study what theology is – its greatness and its aporias, its opportunities and its dead ends. And here by theology I mean not only the theology that is actually being done today but also what theology could be. In these windows, too, art has anticipated our reflections and they are only approximately catching up with it.

Let me first explain how the idea came to me that one could use these windows to demonstrate what theology is.

My first impression of the designs was ambivalent. At that time the overall plan wasn't known, and only designs for a few individual windows were available. What disturbed me was the constant recurrence of writing: in quotations, letter and manuscript pages. I missed pictorial elements in the real sense, e.g. the indication of a human face or a symbol like the cross. Of course I told myself, 'You're an exegete, occupied all day in interpreting writing. This "scripture" is the element in which you live. And it stands at the centre of Protestant piety. Why shouldn't the so-called scriptural principle be given artistic form? I had no theological or intellectual objections to this. But in my heart I told myself, 'Perhaps the artist simply has limitations. Perhaps he keeps using the same idea because he hasn't any others.' Like scholars who keep varying the same idea in their articles, engaged in scientific recycling, so too there may be artists who keep using a good idea like a theme with many variations.

My reservations were overcome when for the first time I saw a description of the overall plan. It dawned on me that what had first seemed 'poverty of ideas' was in fact one idea with great inner richness. The programme according to which the pictures were designed quite deliberately embraces all the sign systems, all the forms of notation that human beings have developed. Speech and language have a privileged place among them, as they have a privileged place in our religion.

But alongside them we find other sign languages:
Computer print-outs
Chemical formulae like that for the structure of penicillin
Mathematical and physical formulae like $E = mc^2$
Musical notation and scores
Maps
Architectural plans (of churches)
Traffic signs
Television pictures
A weather chart
Curves like those of an electrocardiogram

And in addition to that, time and again script – or writings, references to philosophical and poetical works, quotations from the Bible, promises, prayers. All in many languages. Here beyond question there is a deliberate intent. All sign language is to be represented. The windows are meant to be an impressive 'semiotic symphony', i.e. a composition using different sign languages.

'But what has theology to do with this?' you may rightly ask. Wouldn't the Heidelberg window designs have been more suitable for an institute for semiotics or linguistics, if the theory of signs is regarded as the basic science of linguistics? My claim is that they are theology through and through; indeed they are quite grandiose theology.

Let me demonstrate this by a parable. Imagine that you've been cast ashore on a desert island – either through shipwreck or in the course of an expedition. The island seems wild and uninhabited. You go into the interior. There on the ground you discover a regular triangle of stones. You immediately recognize that it's a sign, and at the same time you say:

1. Behind this lies the intention of communicating something or asking for something.

2. You are not alone on the island. Other intelligent living beings must also be there – human beings.

The only presupposition is that you find a configuration of quite normal things which as a whole is improbable and simple – and differs from a less ordered background only by virtue of this simplicity and improbability.

Suppose that not only you but an intelligent creature like a rat came by the triangle. I choose the rat, because psychological experiments today have convinced us that there is a certain image of the rat in human beings. This rat sees the same stones. But it cannot interpret them as a sign. At most one could train the rat by 'classical conditioning' to see the triangle sign as a catalyst for a certain form of behaviour: looking for food, if one regularly put bacon on the stone triangle.

Thus far the parable. Now its theological significance. We all come into this world as on to a strange island. We don't know whether we are alone in this giant cosmos. But as they go through the world, some sensitive people are struck by signs, improbable configurations of normal things. Indeed, these people experience the whole world as a sign and a parable of something else, of God. They suspect that they are not alone in this world. A superior, incomprehensible 'intelligence' is at work in it. Everything is a sign that points to this intelligence. Others see the same constellations – but do not experience them as signs. So modern men and women, who are convinced of the image of the rat in human beings, find it difficult to experience this world as a sign. However, those who are convinced that they are in the image of God will find signs pointing to God everywhere. Faith is 'sensitivity to signs'. Faith is such a great sensitivity to signs that even reality as a whole can become a sign – against the background of the greatest chaos imaginable, against the background of the nothingness from which everything was created. For faith, even the simple fact that something exists and nothing does not exist becomes the sign of a power which creates being out of nothingness.

Theologians dispute whether this sensitivity to signs is basically present in everyone, but often covered over and underdeveloped, or whether it is given to people as a result of special experiences – through revelation. One of the advantages of art is that it does not have to confront such alternatives. The Heidelberg window designs do not talk about signs but present them. And the basic notion is that all the sign systems with which people can construct and decipher, and with which they depict reality, point to God. They all point to eternity. And conversely, where God speaks to human beings, God makes use of human sign system, the language of the Bible and religion, and human beings respond with praise and gratitude, lamentation and prayers.

In the nave windows we find above all the first movement: human sign systems become transparent for God's reality. In the choir we find the opposite movement: God speaks to human beings – and they answer in their manifold languages.

The *medicine window* – probably the best-known design, which was exhibited at the Frankfurt Kirchentag in 1987 – is a good example of the transparency of human sign systems. It depicts the heartbeats of an embryo and a dying person. The electrocardiogram becomes the symbol for human life and its finitude. We are usually born in a hospital, surrounded by medicine. And we usually die in one. Here our modern experience of finitude is depicted and dealt with. In the shadows in the bottom right-hand corner early designs had a chemical formula, the formula for penicillin. It stands against a background the colour of which recalls charred paper, that depicts death. What I understand by this is that penicillin – one of the most effective medicines in prolonging the average life-span – cannot in the end protect us from death. Modern medicine can help us to live longer, and also more intensely, and that is quite marvellous. But it makes the experience of finitude and mortality all the more evident. In the window this life is enclosed within two spots of blue. Up above we recognize an asterisk, the generally recognized sign for a birth. This is matched by the cross at the end of the ECG. The heartbeat ceases with death. But the line hasn't come to an end. On the contrary, it is extended as a blue line and ends in a marvellous strip of 'blue', which begins only beyond the ECG. It isn't difficult to interpret this. We come from God's hand and we return to God's hand. Each time, the blue points to the basic limit situation of birth and death. Therefore the blue involuntary directs our gaze back to the birth asterisk – above at a higher level, beyond the ECG. And now perhaps it may strike you that the heart curve of the embryo is not set against a beige background but directly on a red background. Is this meant to indicate that the origin of life is the symbol of a new life beyond death, of which we know as little as the embryos in the womb know of the life that awaits them? And doesn't this picture say even more? Above the whole of life stands the promise of rebirth – a rebirth even now, in the midst of life.

The ECG window is a marvellous symbol of our life, our life between cradle and grace. A few letters, 4 September 1965, give it yet another dimension. That is the date of Albert Schweitzer's death. So here is a new message: what is decisive for our life between cradle and grave is not physical existence, but what we have done in this life. Albert Schweitzer lived a full life – in the service of science, theology, mission, art – but above all in the service of his suffering fellow human beings. So when confronted with this window we involuntarily ask ourselves, 'What are you doing with your life? What are you doing with the time between cradle and grave? What is you life worth if you haven't done something for the least among your brother and sisters?' However, a Jewish anecdote also occurred to me: 'Before the end Rabbi Sussya said, "In the coming world I shall not be asked, 'Why were you not Moses?' I shall be asked, 'Why were you not Sussya?'"' Indeed. Not everyone can be Albert Schweitzer. But we can all be ourselves.

It is easy to understand why this medical window was chosen for the 1989 Berlin Kirchentag as a symbol of its slogan, 'Our time in God's hand'. That wasn't done to offend the people in Heidelberg who have protested so vigorously against these windows, but because this window is convincing and successful. The invitations to the Kirchentag contained a diagram with a representation of the window and a short text for meditation:

> My heart beats! I am alive!
> Where do I come from?
> Where am I going?
> What is the meaning of my life?
>
> Whether or not all is well with me,
> God embraces my life with his faithfulness.
> Birth and death, every day and all time
> are in your hands.
>
> Fill the time that you give me, God,
> with trust and courage, with hope and love.

Let's now look briefly at the biology window. It shows the basic structure of all life, the so-called double helix, consisting of DNS and RNS, deoxyribonucleic acid and ribonucleic acid. Here we do not have a depiction of the irreplaceable individual life but the formula for life generally. We all have a share in a giant stream of life. This life as a whole is threatened. The traces of burning on the edge of the paper show that. Two things should be emphasized. First the spiral shows a movement from below upwards. This sense of direction is produced by the way in which the paper is ragged at the top while it has a straight border at the bottom. Anyone can sense that the formula of life is going further, that it really should have reached up into the red of the tracery above. Furthermore, the double helix seems to open towards its red background. The red background becomes visible in the midst of life. As red is the colour of divine reality – one need think only of the medicine window – we may understand this to indicate that the language of the creator may be perceived in the basic structure of life. Certainly many people see life only as an improbable organization of matter and molecules. However, for faith, God's reality shines through the basic structure of life. The whole stream of life is on its way to God. Indeed, for me the whole of life, from the slipper animalcule to *homo sapiens*, is a process of trial and error on the way to God, a hypothesis, corrected time and again, which seeks to correspond to God. And in us this process has reached consciousness of itself. As representatives of all life we have responsibility for this stream of life in which we ourselves stand.

So much for the human sign systems, which in the window designs become pointers to God. Here to some degree we have a 'theology from below'. The whole composition of the window designs shows that the other movement, the movement from above downwards – from God's word to the human answer – precedes this movement from below upwards.

Look once again at the basic plan. On the left of the choir, windows are planned to represent signs through which God speaks to human beings: creation, Torah and prophets, the Beatitudes – i.e. God's promise to human beings. On the right of the choir the human answer is depicted.

Plan of the Heidelberg window designs of Johannes Schreiter

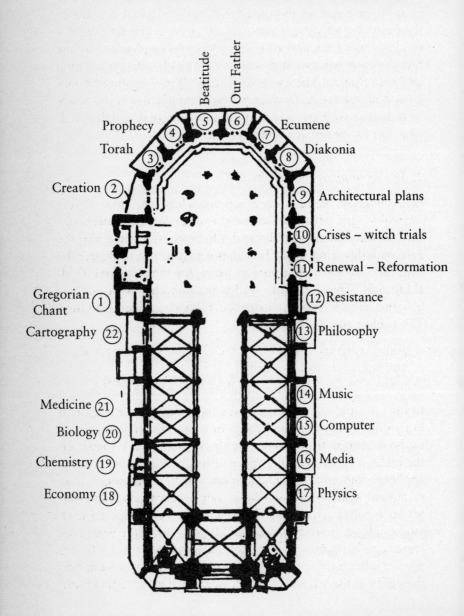

This answer comprises: first, prayer in the Our Father window; then the ecumene – the multiplicity of churches and religions in this world; diakonia, i.e. help for the weak and handicapped; and finally the church as the place of worship in the form of synagogue, catacomb and church. The ambivalence of all human responses to God's address is emphasized by the fact that one window is devoted to crises (the wars of religion and the 'criminal history of Christianity') and another to constant renewal, the *ecclesia semper reformanda*. But at the centre of the choir we have a juxtaposition of the two middle windows. Let's look rather more closely at them.

1. *The window of the Beatitude s*

Some window designs have aspects which are immediately accessible, and others which only emerge through interpretation (in some cases by additional information). That is also the case with this window. At first glance anyone can recognize the Beatitude 'Blessed... the pure in heart, for they shall see God' (Matt.5.8). This Beatitude is closely connected with another promise, with Jesus' promise to the 'robber' crucified with him. The robber asks Jesus,

'Jesus, remember me when you come into your kingdom',
And Jesus said to him, 'truly I tell you,
Today you will be with me in paradise' (Luke 23.42f.).

In my view the combination of the two promises – the general one in the Sermon on the Mount to all and the individual one to the robber on the cross – is highly significant. The robber on the cross was certainly not 'pure in heart', but Jesus' promise applies to him, too. That makes it possible to apply this promise to anyone – including us, who certainly hesitate to claim that we have pure hearts. Now between the two promises we see a strip of blood. Individual drops of blood run over the Beatitude. Here is an indication why not only the innocent, those who are pure of heart, may apply Jesus' promise to themselves – but also the guilty, those who have failed. According to Christian faith, this is made possible by the cross. The window designs clearly contradict any tendency to separate Jesus' preaching from his fate, any tendency just to take over the proclamation of the forgiveness of sins but to shelve the reconciliation by the cross as an outdated idea. In these window designs we are not confronted with a 'modern theology' which in perplexity is trying to reinterpret the great images of faith. Rather, these images are made to speak. This theology is more 'conservative'. It seeks to preserve Christian identity in the midst of our time.

The pictograms which serve as traffic signs are also relatively easy to interpret. They are meant to be commandment signs, orientations for human beings. Let's begin at the bottom right: there a round sign points in all four directions. Does this seek to say that God gives human beings the freedom to break out in all directions – where they will? They have the possibility of moving away from God, and indeed they do. But they can also use this freedom in quite a different way: they can use it to go into all the world, to bring the word of Jesus to all nations. The very next sign, rather further to the left, already introduces a new element. Human beings can change direction. They can reverse, in order to take the way upwards. The promise guides them in a new direction. The next rectangular sign links the lower third of the window to the upper third. It extends up into the dialogue between Jesus and the robber. Perhaps it is meant to depict both Jesus and the robber on a shared way upwards. But it is illuminating that the sense of direction is still open. The parallel signs can be interpreted as ways which can be taken in both directions. That is not the case with the sign above – another sign that links various fields in the window. Here we are clearly told, 'One way only' – upwards. The reference is to Jesus, who, as the Gospel of John says, is himself the way, the truth and the life. In the tracery above we then find another round sign, this time blue. We recall the blue in the medicine window. Here is an indication that the goal is attained, the vision of God. For that is the leading thought behind this window, 'Blessed are the pure in heart, for they will see God.'

We need some information about the two manuscripts in the

centre of the picture. Here we have a Greek manuscript of the
New Testament, the so-called Codex Sinaiticus, from which the
page containing the Beatitude of the Sermon on the Mount is
depicted. Below it we find the same Beatitude in Hebrew. That is
very interesting. The New Testament has not been transmitted to
us in Hebrew in ancient codices. But we know that Jesus himself
spoke Hebrew (or Aramaic). Behind the Greek of the New Testament there is (probably) an Aramaic tradition in the Gospels.
Here the window design conveys very simply that the story of
Jesus is part of Jewish history. Today, more than ever, we are
aware that all of Christianity has Jewish roots. That is expressed
here in an elementary way, just as Chagall expressed it in his way
when he kept depicting Jesus in conjunction with persecuted and
suffering Jews. Schreiter's window designs seem to me to be a
Christian response to the great art of the Jew Chagall. One might
also think of the window on which architectural plans of a
church and a synagogue are to stand side by side.

Perhaps you have been struck by seeing a single drop of blood
in the Hebrew text. It stands in the middle of the Beatitude on
the peacemakers. Is this meant to express the fact that Jesus
himself is the one who has made peace – between Jews and
Gentiles 'through his cross', as it says in Ephesians (Eph. 2.14-
16)? Is this a reminder that the promise applies to those who are
persecuted? Or are our thoughts being directed to the disastrous
history of Christian anti-Judaism? There are many possibilities
here, and I think that we should allow our thoughts to be drawn
in different directions. For the windows as a whole are like those
which contain broken texts. This offends some people. But it
contains an indication for us: as onlookers we ourselves have to
fill in the lines; we may find the meaning of what is depicted for
ourselves, and often there are several readings!

2. *The Our Father window*

Let's now take a look at the second window, which depicts the
human response in prayer. Here, too, some things are easy to
interpret. We immediately recognize the petition from the Lord's

Prayer, 'Forgive us our trespasses, as we forgive those who trespass against us.' And again this petition, which has been handed down, along with the Lord's Prayer, in the Beatitudes, is connected with a scene from the passion narrative, the scene in Gethsemane. In strips of text above the blood-red colour we read:

'Father, if you are willing, remove this cup from me; yet, not my will but yours be done. And his sweat became like great drops of blood falling down on the ground' (Luke 22.42,44).

The artist has put the drops of blood as red spots in the middle of the text.

The combination of the two prayers, the prayer of Jesus and the Our Father, is quite deliberate. For the Our Father begins with a relative clause, 'who art'. The address 'Father' must be supplied from the Gethsemane prayer above. And again the blood flowing down depicts what for Christian faith is the basis of the forgiveness of sins: the cross of Christ. But the way in which the petition begins abruptly with the relative periphrasis 'who art' also prompts further thoughts. The 'who art' now takes the place of a form of address. God is addressed as the one who exists. Those who are familiar with their Bibles will immediately think of God's revelation of himself in the burning bush. There God introduces himself as 'I am who I am' (Ex.3.14). God also uses this name in addressing Moses. So the one who is addressed in the Our Father appears as the same God who has disclosed himself in the history of Israel. It might be mentioned in passing that these connections can be made only in translation, and not in the original text of the Our Father, but this fact is irrelevant to the interpretation.

Let's now look at the pictograms. Again the sign at the bottom right depicts the human situation; this time, however, not the human possibility of going in all directions but the human conflict, made vivid by two arrows pointing at each other. This is an indication of the conflict between God's will and the human will, a conflict which is also expressed in the Gethsemane prayer, 'Not my will but yours be done.' It is no coincidence that the other rectangular sign stands under the words 'as we'. It possibly shows two people who have forgiven each other. They stand turned to each other – as open brackets – like hands which are opening. However, the decisive thing is that here the open side of the brackets does not yet point upwards. This upward pointer only appears in the sign in the upper third of the window – a symbol of the receiving of divine forgiveness. Finally, the same bracket with the open side upwards appears yet again at the top of the tracery. Now, together with the top of the rosette it forms an arrow. The blue colour indicates that here the way is at an end. Here the goal is near.

Most of the window is taken up with representations of the Lord's Prayer in seven languages:

English – right at the top as the *lingua franca* of our world
Eritrean
Russian
Chinese
Arabic
Spanish
Sanskrit.

The languages represent all the continents: Europe, Asia, Africa, America and Australia. But not only that. The languages of the old high religions have deliberately been chosen: Sanskrit stands for Hinduism, Chinese for Buddhism and Confucianism, Arabic for Islam. Judaism was already represented in the left-hand window. As mediator of the promise it has a special role. What the window is saying is that the human response to this promise takes place in many languages, indeed in many religions. In fact the Our Father is a prayer in which many non-Christians can join.

3. *The relationship between the windows*

The two windows are closely related to each other. Let me make that clear once again. A band of text runs through both windows. Here it is striking that if the basic theme of the left-hand window is Jesus' promise to human beings and the basic theme of the right-hand window is the human response, in the band of text this opposition is overcome. For the left-hand window also contains the robber with his request: the baneful criminal on the cross raises his voice in the midst of the Beatitudes. Similarly, in the right-hand window Jesus himself is depicted as the one who prays. The one who formulates the promise and extends it to human beings now himself appears on the human side – as a man in anxiety and fear of death.

This bond between the left-hand and right-hand windows is emphasized by the band of blood which runs through them. Both the promise and the human answer are made possible by the suffering of Christ. This strip of blood has a clear sense of direction: the drops of blood are falling downwards. They are formed as though they are caught up in a great upheaval which restricts their 'natural' downward course – an indication not only of the earthquake at the crucifixion, but also of the shattering effect of any suffering. But even if one doesn't perceive this directly, one grasps the movement 'downwards'. The pictograms indicate a directly opposed movement. They point from below upwards. They point to a second red strip – as if blood had changed into blessing and pain into beauty. Note that even the signs pointing upwards all display the red colour of blood.

Finally note the feature which brackets the two windows together. Jesus' promise and the human answer are to be seen in close conjunction. The two belong together. This bracket is basically the same element that also occurs in three pictograms of the right-hand window: three signs which seem to me to indicate that forgiveness bridges the gulf between God and human beings – and similarly the distance and the hostility between human beings.

The drops of blood in the choir window represent in a restrained way the crucifix which stands in all churches. Familiarity hardly allows us to see these crucifixes for what they are: representations of a tormented and tortured man. By depicting only drops of blood, this window communicates the deviation from the customary far more powerfully than the direct depiction of pain and torment. Jesus is more present in this indirect form than elsewhere. He is not present as image, but present as word. He is active in his church through his words: through the Beatitudes and the Our Father This word is illuminated in the morning by the sun as it rises in the east. It cast its light into the bloodstained depths of human life. It gives orientation and points upwards – to God.

Perhaps you can now understand why I think that the Heidelberg window designs are theological through and through. This symphony in human sign languages has just a single theme: human beings before God and God's word before human beings. These windows represent a grandiose music of signs in honour of God, a music of signs in which the dissonances of human life ring out in powerful harmony, but the light of reconciliation – in the marvellously warm red – penetrates to every abyss. Here we can learn what theology is. So I can well imagine that one open day we shall be able to use them to show what we are really seeking to do in the theological faculty. If a committee again has to rack its brains about how it can make clear what theology is to the general public, to school-leavers or to new students, one could show these windows. They would be a great help in beginning a conversation. If they could be seen one day in the Holy Spirit Church, I would go there with students from our nearby Theological Seminar. There one could demonstrate in a very simple way that theology cannot be studied if one does not also experience the church from within. Seen from outside, some 'windows' may barely work. But seen from within they shine out in the most marvellous colours like these window designs by Johannes Schreiter.